BLACK

POWER

The Politics of
Liberation in America

BLACK

POWER

The Politics
of Liberation
in America

STOKELY CARMICHAEL
& CHARLES V. HAMILTON

VINTAGE BOOKS   New York

A DIVISION OF RANDOM HOUSE

VINTAGE BOOKS

are published by ALFRED A. KNOPF, INC.

and RANDOM HOUSE, INC.

The authors wish to thank the following for permission to quote material which appears in this volume:
The New Republic: quotations from "A Time to be Black," by Bruce Detweiler, © 1966 by Harrison-Blaine of New Jersey, Inc.; from "Accommodating Whites: A New Look at Mississippi," by Christopher Jencks, © 1966 by Harrison-Blaine of New Jersey, Inc.; *The Tuskegee News:* quotations from a letter to the editor, January 20, 1966; *The National Review:* quotations from "Organized Labor and the Negro Worker," by Myra Bain (June 4, 1963): *Hill and Wang, Inc.:* quotations from *From Plantation to Ghetto* by August Meier and Elliot Rudwick; *The Nation:* quotations from "Murder in Tuskegee: Day of Wrath on the Model Town," by Arnold Kaufman (January 31, 1966); *Saturday Evening Post:* quotations from "A New White Backlash," (September 10, 1966); Professor Kenneth Clark, *Ebony* magazine, and Harper and Row, Inc.: quotations from "What Motivates American Whites," from *Ebony* magazine, © 1966 by Johnson Publishing Co., Inc., and from *Dark Ghetto* (Harper & Row, Inc., 1965); Random House, Inc.: quotations from *Crisis in Black and White,* by Charles Silberman. © 1964 by Random House, Inc.; Prentice-Hall, Inc.: quotations from *Racial Crisis in America: Leadership in Conflict,* by Lewis Killian and Charles Grigg. 1964; quotations from *The Negro Leadership Class,* by Daniel Thompson, © 1963; quotations from *The American Negro Reference Book,* edited by John P. Davis, © 1966.

Manufactured in the United States of America

This book is dedicated to our mothers, Mrs. Mabel Carmichael (affectionately known as May Charles) and Mrs. Viola White, and to all the black mothers who have struggled through the centuries so that this generation could fight for black power

This book presents a political framework and ideology which represents the last reasonable opportunity for this society to work out its racial problems short of prolonged destructive guerrilla warfare. That such violent warfare may be unavoidable is not herein denied. But if there is the slightest chance to avoid it, the politics of Black Power as described in this book is seen as the only viable hope.

STOKELY CARMICHAEL,
CHARLES V. HAMILTON
AUGUST 1967

PREFACE

❶ This book is about why, where and in what manner black people in America must get themselves together. It is about black people taking care of business—the business of and for black people. The stakes are really very simple: if we fail to do this, we face continued subjection to a white society that has no intention of giving up willingly or easily its position of priority and authority. If we succeed, we will exercise control over our lives, politically, economically and psychically. We will also contribute to the development of a viable larger society; in terms of ultimate social benefit, there is nothing unilateral about the movement to free black people.

We present no pat formulas in this book for ending racism. We do not offer a blueprint; we cannot set any timetables for freedom. This is not a handbook for the working organizer; it will not tell him exactly how to proceed in day-to-day decision-making. If we tried to do any of those things, our book would be useless and literally dead within a year or two. For the rules are being changed constantly. Black communities are using different means, including armed rebellion, to achieve their ends. Out of these various experiments come programs. This is our experience: programs do not come out of the minds of any one person or two people such as ourselves, but out of day-to-day work, out of interaction between organizers and the communities in which they work.

Therefore our aim is to offer a framework. We are calling here for broad experimentation in accordance with the concept of Black Power, and we will suggest certain guidelines, certain specific examples of such experiments. We start with the assumption that in order to get the right answers, one must pose the right questions. In order to find effective solutions, one must formulate the problem correctly. One must start from premises rooted in truth and reality rather than myth.

In addition, we aim to define and encourage a new consciousness among black people which will make it possible for us to proceed toward those answers and those solutions. This consciousness, which will be defined more fully in Chapter II, might be called a sense of peoplehood: pride, rather than shame, in blackness, and an attitude of brotherly, communal responsibility among all black people for one another.

To ask the right questions, to encourage a new consciousness and to suggest new forms which express it: these are the basic purposes of our book.

It follows that there are statements in this book which most whites and some black people would prefer not to hear. The whole question of race is one that America would much rather not face honestly and squarely. To some, it is embarrassing; to others, it is inconvenient; to still others, it is confusing. But for black Americans, to know it and tell it like it is and then to act on that knowledge should be neither embarrassing nor inconvenient nor confusing. Those responses are luxuries for people with time to spare, who feel no particular sense of urgency about the need to solve certain serious social problems. Black people in America have no time to play nice, polite parlor games— especially when the lives of *their* children are at stake. Some white Americans can afford to speak softly, tread lightly, employ the soft-sell and put-off (or is it put-down?). They own the society. For black people to adopt *their* methods of relieving *our* oppression is ludicrous. We blacks must respond in our own way, on our own terms, in a manner which fits our temperaments. The definitions of ourselves, the roles we pursue, the goals we seek are *our* responsibility.

It is crystal clear that the society is capable of and willing to reward those individuals who do not forcefully condemn it—to reward them with prestige, status and material benefits. But these crumbs of co-optation should be rejected. The over-riding, all-important fact is that *as a people*, we have absolutely nothing to lose by refusing to play such games.

Camus and Sartre have asked: Can a man condemn himself? Can whites, particularly liberal whites, condemn themselves? Can they stop blaming blacks and start blaming their own system? Are they capable of the shame which might become a revolutionary emotion? We—black people —have found that they usually cannot condemn themselves; therefore black Americans must do it. (We also offer, in Chapter III of this book, our ideas of what whites can do who want to be helpful.)

Anything less than clarity, honesty and forcefulness perpetuates the centuries of sliding over, dressing up, and soothing down the true feelings, hopes and demands of an oppressed black people. Mild demands and hypocritical smiles mislead white America into thinking that all is

fine and peaceful. They mislead white America into thinking that the path and pace chosen to deal with racial problems are acceptable to masses of black Americans. It is far
better to speak forcefully and truthfully. Only when one's
true self—white or black—is exposed, can this society proceed to deal with the problems from a position of clarity
and not from one of misunderstanding.

Thus we have no intention of engaging in the rather
meaningless language so common to discussions of race in
America: "Granted, things were and are bad, but we are
making progress"; "Granted, your demands are legitimate,
but we cannot move hastily. Stable societies are best built
slowly"; "Be careful that you do not anger or alienate your
white allies; remember, after all, you are only ten percent of
the population." We reject this language and these views,
whether expressed by black or white; we leave them to
others to mouth, because we do not feel that this rhetoric
is either relevant or useful.

Rather, we would suggest a more meaningful language,
that of Frederick Douglass, a black American who understood the nature of protest in this society:

> Those who profess to favor freedom yet deprecate agita-
> tion, are men who want crops without plowing up the
> ground; they want rain without thunder and lightning. They
> want the ocean without the awful roar of its many waters.
> . . . Power concedes nothing without demand. It never did
> and it never will. Find out just what any people will quietly
> submit to and you have found out the exact measure of in-
> justice and wrong which will be imposed upon them, and
> these will continue till they are resisted with either words
> or blow, or with both. The limits of tyrants are prescribed
> by the endurance of those whom they oppress.[1]

Finally, it should be noted that this book does not discuss at length the international situation, the relationship

[1] West India Emancipation Speech, August, 1857.

of our black liberation struggle to the rest of the world. But Black Power means that black people see themselves as part of a new force, sometimes called the "Third World"; that we see our struggle as closely related to liberation struggles around the world. We must hook up with these struggles. We must, for example, ask ourselves: when black people in Africa begin to storm Johannesburg, what will be the role of this nation—and of black people here? It seems inevitable that this nation would move to protect its financial interests in South Africa, which means protecting white rule in South Africa. Black people in this country then have the responsibility to oppose, at least to neutralize, that effort by white America.

This is but one example of many such situations which have already arisen around the world—with more to come. There is only one place for black Americans in these struggles, and that is on the side of the Third World. Frantz Fanon, in *The Wretched of the Earth*, puts forth clearly the reasons for this and the relationship of the concept called Black Power to the concept of a new force in the world:

> Let us decide not to imitate Europe; let us try to create the whole man, whom Europe has been incapable of bringing to triumphant birth.
>
> Two centuries ago, a former European colony decided to catch up with Europe. It succeeded so well that the United States of America became a monster, in which the taints, the sickness and the inhumanity of Europe have grown to appalling dimensions. . . .
>
> The Third World today faces Europe like a colossal mass whose aim should be to try to resolve the problems to which Europe has not been able to find the answers . . .
>
> It is a question of the Third World starting a new history of Man, a history which will have regard to the sometimes prodigious theses which Europe has put forward, but which will also not forget Europe's crimes, of which the most horrible was committed in the heart of man, and consisted of

the pathological tearing apart of his functions and the crumbling away of his unity.

No, there is no question of a return to nature. It is simply a very concrete question of not dragging men towards mutilation, of not imposing upon the brain rhythms which very quickly obliterate it and wreck it. The pretext of catching up must not be used to push man around, to tear him away from himself or from his privacy, to break and kill him.

No, we do not want to catch up with anyone. What we want to do is go forward all the time, night and day, in the company of Man, in the company of all men . . . [pp. 253–55].

Our thanks to Ivanhoe Donaldson, *who made a major contribution in Chapter* VII, *to SNCC and to all the people in the struggle with whom we worked, for their help, insights and strength in the formation and articulation of the ideas presented in this book.*

CONTENTS

BLACK

POWER

The Politics of Liberation in America

WHITE POWER:

The dark ghettos are social, political, educational and—above all—economic colonies. Their inhabitants are subject peoples, victims of the greed, cruelty, insensitivity, guilt, and fear of their masters.

DR. KENNETH B. CLARK,
Dark Ghetto, p. 11.*

In an age of decolonization, it may be fruitful to regard the problem of the American Negro as a unique case of

* In order to avoid excessive bibliographical footnoting, the authors have provided such footnotes only where the source is a monograph, periodical, newspaper, etc. In the case of book sources, the title, author and page reference will be found together with the quoted material, in the body of the text. A bibliography at the back of this book will provide the reader with publisher, place and date of publication.

The Colonial Situation

colonialism, an instance of internal imperialism, an under-developed people in our very midst.

I. F. STONE,
The New York Review of Books
(August 18, 1966), p. 10.

◗ What is racism? The word has represented daily reality to millions of black people for centuries, yet it is rarely defined—perhaps just because that reality has been such a commonplace. By "racism" we mean the predication of decisions and policies on considerations of race for the purpose of *subordinating* a racial group and maintaining control over that group. That has been the practice of this country toward the black man; we shall see why and how.

Racism is both overt and covert. It takes two, closely related forms: individual whites acting against individual blacks, and acts by the total white community against the black community. We call these individual racism and institutional racism. The first consists of overt acts by individuals, which cause death, injury or the violent destruction of property. This type can be recorded by television cameras; it can frequently be observed in the process of commission. The second type is less overt, far more subtle, less identifiable in terms of *specific* individuals committing the acts. But it is no less destructive of human life. The second type originates in the operation of established and respected forces in the society, and thus receives far less public condemnation than the first type.

When white terrorists bomb a black church and kill five black children, that is an act of individual racism, widely deplored by most segments of the society. But when in that same city—Birmingham, Alabama—five hundred black babies die each year because of the lack of proper food, shelter and medical facilities, and thousands more are destroyed and maimed physically, emotionally and intellectually because of conditions of poverty and discrimination in the black community, that is a function of institutional racism. When a black family moves into a home in a white neighborhood and is stoned, burned or routed out, they are victims of an overt act of individual racism which many people will condemn—at least in words. But it is institutional racism that keeps black people locked in dilapidated slum tenements, subject to the daily prey of exploitative slumlords, merchants, loan sharks and discriminatory real estate agents. The society either pretends it does not know of this latter situation, or is in fact incapable of doing anything meaningful about it. We shall examine the reasons for this in a moment.

Institutional racism relies on the active and pervasive operation of anti-black attitudes and practices. A sense of superior group position prevails: whites are "better" than blacks; therefore blacks should be subordinated to whites. This is a racist attitude and it permeates the society, on both the individual and institutional level, covertly and overtly.

"Respectable" individuals can absolve themselves from individual blame: *they* would never plant a bomb in a church; *they* would never stone a black family. But they continue to support political officials and institutions that would and do perpetuate institutionally racist policies. Thus *acts* of overt, individual racism may not typify the society, but institutional racism does—with the support of covert, individual *attitudes* of racism. As Charles Silberman wrote, in *Crisis in Black and White,*

> What we are discovering, in short, is that the United States—all of it, North as well as South, West as well as East—is a racist society in a sense and to a degree that we have refused so far to admit, much less face. . . . The tragedy of race relations in the United States is that there is no American Dilemma. White Americans are not torn and tortured by the conflict between their devotion to the American creed and their actual behavior. They are upset by the current state of race relations, to be sure. But what troubles them is not that justice is being denied but that their peace is being shattered and their business interrupted [pp. 9–10].

To put it another way, there is no "American dilemma" because black people in this country form a colony, and it is not in the interest of the colonial power to liberate them. Black people are legal citizens of the United States with, for the most part, the same *legal* rights as other citizens. Yet they stand as colonial subjects in relation to the white society. Thus institutional racism has another name: colonialism.

Obviously, the analogy is not perfect. One normally associates a colony with a land and people subjected to, and physically separated from, the "Mother Country." This is not always the case, however; in South Africa and Rhodesia, black and white inhabit the same land—with blacks subordinated to whites just as in the English, French, Italian, Portuguese and Spanish colonies. It is the objective relationship which counts, not rhetoric (such as constitutions *articulating* equal rights) or geography.

The analogy is not perfect in another respect. Under classic colonialism, the colony is a source of cheaply produced raw materials (usually agricultural or mineral) which the "Mother Country" then processes into finished goods and sells at high profit—sometimes back to the colony itself. The black communities of the United States do not export anything except human labor. But is the differentiation more than a technicality? Essentially, the African colony is selling its labor; the product itself does not belong to the "subjects" because the land is not theirs. At the same time, let us look at the black people of the South: cultivating cotton at $3.00 for a ten-hour day and from that buying cotton dresses (and food and other goods) from white manufacturers. Economists might wish to argue this point endlessly; the objective relationship stands. Black people in the United States have a colonial relationship to the larger society, a relationship characterized by institutional racism. That colonial status operates in three areas—political, economic, social—which we shall discuss one by one.

■

Colonial subjects have their political decisions made for them by the colonial masters, and those decisions are handed down directly or through a process of "indirect rule." Politically, decisions which affect black lives have always been made by white people—the "white power structure." There is some dislike for this phrase because it tends to ignore or oversimplify the fact that there are many centers of power, many different forces making decisions. Those who raise that objection point to the pluralistic character of the body politic. They frequently overlook the fact that American pluralism quickly becomes a monolithic structure on issues of race. When faced with demands from black people, the multi-faction whites unite and present a common front. This is especially true when the black group increases in number: ". . . a large Negro population is politically both an asset and a liability. A large Negro populace may not only expect to influence the commitments and behavior of a governor, but it also may expect to arouse the fears of many whites. The larger the Negro population, the greater the perceived threat (in the eyes of whites) and thus the greater the resistance to broad civil rights laws." [1]

Again, the white groups tend to view their interests in a particularly united, solidified way when confronted with blacks making demands which are seen as threatening to vested interests. The whites react in a united group to protect interests they perceive to be theirs—interests possessed to the exclusion of those who, for varying reasons, are outside the group. Professor Robin M. Williams, Jr. has summed up the situation:

In a very basic sense, "race relations" are the direct outgrowth of the long wave of European expansion, beginning with the discovery of America. Because of their more highly developed technology and economic and political organization, the Europeans were able by military force or by eco-

[1] James Q. Wilson, "The Negro in American Politics: The Present," *The American Negro Reference Book* (ed. by John P. Davis), Englewood Cliffs, New Jersey: Prentice-Hall, 1966, p 453.

nomic and political penetration to secure control over colonies, territories, protectorates and other possessions and spheres of influence around the world. In a way, the resulting so-called race relations had very little to do with "race" —initially it was an historical accident that the peoples encountered in the European expansion differed in shared physical characteristics of an obvious kind. *But once the racial ideologies had been formed and widely disseminated, they constituted a powerful means of justifying political hegemony and economic control.*

In much the same way, present-day vested political, economic and social privileges and rights tend to be rationalized and defended by persons and groups who hold such prerogatives.

. . . Whenever a number of persons within a society have enjoyed for a considerable period of time certain opportunities for getting wealth, for exercising power and authority, and for successfully claiming prestige and social deference, there is a strong tendency for these people to feel that these benefits are theirs "by right." The advantages come to be thought of as normal, proper, customary, as sanctioned by time, precedent and social consensus. Proposals to change the existing situation arouse reactions of "moral indignation." Elaborate doctrines are developed to show the inevitability and rightness of the existing scheme of things.

An established system of vested interests is a powerful thing, perhaps especially when differences in power, wealth and prestige coincide with relatively indelible symbols of collective membership, such as shared hereditary physical traits, a distinctive religion, or a persistently held culture. *The holders of an advantaged position see themselves as a group and reinforce one another in their attitudes; any qualms about the justice of the status quo seem to be diminished by the group character of the arrangements.*[2]

[2] Robin M. Williams, Jr., "Prejudice and Society," *The American Negro Reference Book* (ed. by John P. Davis), Englewood Cliffs, New Jersey: Prentice-Hall, 1966, pp. 727–29.

But what about the official "separation of powers"—the system of "checks and balances"? We are well aware that political power is supposedly divided at the national level between the President, the Congress and the courts. But somehow, the war in Vietnam has proceeded without Congressional approval. We are aware that Constitutional niceties (really, they quickly become irrelevancies) divide power between the Federal Government and the states. But somehow the Supreme Court has found no difficulty in expanding the powers of Congress over interstate commerce. At the same time, we are told that the Federal Government is very limited in what it can do to stop whites from attacking and murdering civil rights workers. A group interest does exist and it crosses all the supposed lines when necessary, thereby rendering them irrelevant. Furthermore, whites frequently see *themselves* as a monolithic group on racial issues and act accordingly.

The black community perceives the "white power structure" in very concrete terms. The man in the ghetto sees his white landlord come only to collect exorbitant rents and fail to make necessary repairs, while both know that the white-dominated city building inspection department will wink at violations or impose only slight fines. The man in the ghetto sees the white policeman on the corner brutally manhandle a black drunkard in a doorway, and at the same time accept a pay-off from one of the agents of the white-controlled rackets. He sees the streets in the ghetto lined with uncollected garbage, and he knows that the powers which could send trucks in to collect that garbage are white. When they don't, he knows the reason: the low political esteem in which the black community is held. He looks at the absence of a meaningful curriculum in the ghetto schools—for example, the history books that woefully overlook the historical achievements of black people —and he knows that the school board is controlled by whites.[3] He is not about to listen to intellectual discourses on the pluralistic and fragmented nature of political power. He is faced with a "white power structure" as monolithic as Europe's colonial offices have been to African and Asian colonies.

There is another aspect of colonial politics frequently found in colonial Africa and in the United States: the process of indirect rule. Martin Kilson describes it in *Political Change in a West African State, A Study of the Modernization Process in Sierra Leone:* "Indirect rule is the method of local colonial administration through the agency of Chiefs who exercise executive authority. It was applied in one form or other throughout British colonial Africa and was, from the standpoint of the metropolitan power's budget, a form of colonialism-on-the-cheap" (p. 24). In other words, the white power structure rules the black community through local blacks who are responsive to the white leaders, the downtown, white machine, not to the black populace. These black politicians do not exercise effective power. They cannot be relied upon to make forceful demands in behalf of their black constituents, and they become no more than puppets. They put loyalty to a political party before loyalty to their constituents and thus nullify any bargaining power the black community might develop. Colonial politics causes the subject to muffle his voice while participating in the councils of the white power structure. The black man forfeits his opportunity to speak forcefully and clearly for his race, and he justifies this in terms of expediency. Thus, when one talks of a "Negro Establishment" in most places in this country, one is talking of an Estab-

---

[3] Studies have shown the heavy preponderance of business and professional men on school boards throughout the country. One survey showed that such people, although only fifteen percent of the population, constituted seventy-six percent of school board members in a national sample. The percentage of laborers on the boards was only three percent. William C. Mitchell, *The American Polity: A Social and Cultural Interpretation,* Glencoe, Illinois: Free Press, 1962.

lishment resting on a white power base; of hand-picked blacks whom that base projects as showpieces out front. These black "leaders" are, then, only as powerful as their white kingmakers will permit them to be. This is no less true of the North than the South.

Describing the political situation in Chicago, Wilson wrote in *Negro Politics:*

> Particularly annoying to the Negro politicians has been the partial loss of their ability to influence the appointment of Negroes to important or prestigious jobs on public boards and agencies. Negroes selected for membership on such bodies as the Board of Education, the Land Clearance Commission, the Community Conservation Board, the Chicago Plan Commission, and other groups are the "token leaders" . . . and control over their appointment has in part passed out of the Negro machine [p. 84].

Before Congressman William O. Dawson (black Congressman from the predominantly black First Congressional District of Southside Chicago) was co-opted by the white machine, he was an outspoken champion of the race. Afterward, he became a tool of the downtown white Democratic power structure; the black community no longer had an effective representative who would articulate and fight to relieve their grievances. Mr. Dawson became assimiliated. The white political bosses could rule the black community in the same fashion that Britain ruled the African colonies —by indirect rule. Note the result, as described in Silberman's *Crisis in Black and White:*

> Chicago provides an excellent example of how Negroes can be co-opted into inactivity. . . . Dawson surrendered far more than he has obtained for the Negro community. What Dawson obtained were the traditional benefits of the big-city political machine: low-paying jobs for a lot of followers; political intervention with the police and with bail bondsmen, social workers, housing officials, and other bureaucrats whose decisions can affect a poor constituent's life; and a

slice of the "melon" in the form of public housing projects, welfare payments, and the like.

What Dawson surrendered was the pride and dignity of his community; he threw away the opportunity to force Chicago's political and civic leaders to identify and deal with the fundamental problems of segregation and oppression [p. 206].

Dawson, and countless others like him, have an answer to this criticism: this is the proper way to operate; you must "play ball" with the party in order to exact maximum benefits. We reject this notion. It may well result in particular benefits—in terms of status or material gains—for individuals, but it does not speak to the alleviation of a multitude of social problems shared by the masses. They may also say: if I spoke up, I would no longer be permitted to take part in the party councils. I would be ousted, and then the black people would have neither voice nor access. Ultimately, this is, at best, a spurious argument, which does more to enhance the security of the individual person than it does to gain substantial benefits for the group.

In time, one notes that a gap develops between the leadership and the followers. The masses, correctly, no longer view the leaders as their legitimate representatives. They come to see them more for what they are, emissaries sent by the white society. Identity between the two is lost. This frequently occurred in Africa, and the analogy, again, is relevant. Former President of Ghana, Kwame Nkrumah, described the colonial situation in pre-independent Africa in his book *Africa Must Unite:*

The principle of indirect rule adopted in West Africa, and also in other parts of the continent, allowed a certain amount of local self-government in that chiefs could rule their districts provided they did nothing contrary to the laws of the colonial power, and on condition they accepted certain orders from the colonial government. The system of indirect rule was notably successful for a time in Northern Nigeria, where the Emirs governed much as they had done before the colonial period. But the system had obvious dangers. In some cases, autocratic chiefs, propped up by the colonial government, became inefficient and unpopular, as the riots against the chiefs in Eastern Nigeria in 1929, and in Sierra Leone in 1936, showed.

In wide areas of East Africa, where there was no developed system of local government which could be used, headmen or "warrant" chiefs were appointed, usually from noble families. They were so closely tied up with the colonial power that many Africans thought chiefs were an invention of the British [p. 18].

This process of co-optation and a subsequent widening of the gap between the black elites and the masses is common under colonial rule. There has developed in this country an entire class of "captive leaders" in the black communities. These are black people with certain technical and administrative skills who could provide useful leadership roles in the black communities but do not because they have become beholden to the white power structure. These are black school teachers, county agents, junior executives in management positions with companies, etc. In a study of New Orleans contained in Professor Daniel C. Thompson's *The Negro Leadership Class*, public school teachers emerge as the largest professional group in the black community of that city: there were 1,600 of them in 1961. These people are college-trained, articulate, and in daily contact with the young minds of the black South. For the most part (fortunately there are a few exceptions), they are not sources of positive or aggressive community leadership. Thompson concluded:

Depending as they do upon white officials, public school teachers have been greatly restricted in their leadership role . . . several laws passed by the Louisiana State Legislature, as well as rules and regulations adopted by the state and local school boards in recent years, have made it almost impossible for Negro teachers to identify with racial uplift organizations, or even to participate actively in the civil rights movement. This is definitely an important reason why some teachers have remained inactive and silent during heated controversies over civil rights [p. 46].

It is crystal clear that most of these people have accommodated themselves to the racist system. They have capitulated to colonial subjugation in exchange for the security of a few dollars and dubious status. They are effectively lost to the struggle for an improved black position which would fundamentally challenge that racist system. John A. Williams tells in *This is My Country Too* of how he went to Alabama State College (the state college for black people) in 1963 to interview a black professor, who brusquely told him: "Governor Wallace pays my salary; I have nothing to say to you. Excuse me, I have a class to get to" (p. 62).

When black people play colonial politics, they also mislead the white community into thinking that it has the sanction of the blacks. A professor of political science who made a study of black people in Detroit politics from 1956–1960 has concluded:

> The fact that the Negro participates in the system by voting and participating in the party politics in the North should not lead us to conclude that he has accepted the popular consensus of the society about the polity. His support and work for the Democratic party is more a strategic compromise in most cases than a wholehearted endorsement of the party. My own work in Detroit led me to conclude that Negro party officers are not "loyal" to the Democratic party in the way that the ethnic groups or other organized groups such as labor have been. Although the Democratic Party-UAW coalition in Detroit has given the Negro a number of positions in the party hierarchy, it has not included him in the decision-making process.
> . . . As in the colonial situation, the Negro has developed

a submission-aggression syndrome. When he attends campaign strategy meetings he appears to be submissive, willingly accepting the strategies suggested by the white leaders. Despite their seeming acceptance of this condescending treatment, after these meetings the Negro precinct workers will tell you that they had to "go along with all that talk" in order to make sure that they were represented. They openly express their resentment of the party hierarchy and reveal themselves as much more militant about the Negro cause than was apparent during the meeting.[4]

This stance is not an uncommon one. More than a handful of black people will admit privately their contempt for insincere whites with whom they must work and deal. (In all likelihood, the contempt is mutual.) They feel secure in articulating their true feelings only when out of hearing range of "the man."

Those who would assume the responsibility of representing black people in this country must be able to throw off the notion that they can effectively do so and still maintain a maximum amount of security. Jobs will have to be sacrificed, positions of prestige and status given up, favors forfeited. It may well be—and we think it is—that leadership and security are basically incompatible. When one forcefully challenges the racist system, one cannot, at the same time, expect that system to reward him or even treat him comfortably. Political leadership which pacifies and stifles its voice and then rationalizes this on grounds of gaining "something for my people" is, at bottom, gaining only meaningless, token rewards that an affluent society is perfectly willing to give.

A final aspect of political colonialism is the manipulation of political boundaries and the devising of restrictive electoral systems. The point is frequently made that black

[4] A. W. Singham, "The Political Socialization of Marginal Groups." Paper presented at the 1966 annual meeting of the American Political Science Association, New York City.

people are only ten percent of the population—no less a personage than President Johnson has seen fit to remind us of this ratio. It is seldom pointed out that this minority is geographically located so as to create potential majority blocs—that strategic location being an ironic side-effect of segregation. But black people have never been able to utilize fully their numerical voting strength. Where we could vote, the white political machines have gerrymandered black neighborhoods so that the true voting strength is not reflected in political representation. Would anyone looking at the distribution of political power and representation in Manhattan ever think that black people represent sixty percent of the population? On the local level, election to City Councils by the at-large system, rather than by district, reduces the number of representatives coming out of the black community. In Detroit, which uses the at-large system, there was not a black man on the City Council until 1957 despite a vast black population, especially during World War II. Also, the larger the electoral district, the greater the likelihood of there not being a Negro elected because he has to appeal to whites for their votes too. Los Angeles, with very large City Council electoral districts, saw the first black Councilman only in 1963.

The decision-makers are most adept at devising ways or utilizing existing factors to maintain their monopoly of political power.

■

The economic relationship of America's black communities to the larger society also reflects their colonial status. The political power exercised over those communities goes hand in glove with the economic deprivation experienced by the black citizens.

Historically, colonies have existed for the sole purpose of enriching, in one form or another, the "colonizer"; the consequence is to maintain the economic dependency of the "colonized." All too frequently we hear of the missionary motive behind colonization: to "civilize," to "Christianize" the underdeveloped, backward peoples. But read these words of a French Colonial Secretary of State in 1923:

> What is the use of painting the truth? At the start, colonization was not an act of civilization, nor was it a desire to civilize. It was an act of force motivated by interests. An episode in the vital competition which, from man to man, from group to group, has gone on ever increasing; the people who set out to seize colonies in the distant lands were thinking primarily of themselves, and were working for their own profits, and conquering for their own power.[5]

One is immediately reminded of the bitter maxim voiced by many black Africans today: the missionaries came for our goods, not for our good. Indeed, the missionaries turned the Africans' eyes toward heaven, and then robbed them blind in the process. The colonies were sources from which raw materials were taken and markets to which finished products were sold. Manufacture and production were prohibited if this meant—as it usually did—competition with the "mother country." Rich in natural resources, Africa did not reap the benefit of these resources herself. In the Gold Coast (now Ghana), where the cocoa crop was the largest in the world, there was not one chocolate factory.

This same economic status has been perpetrated on the black community in this country. Exploiters come into the ghetto from outside, bleed it dry, and leave it economically dependent on the larger society. As with the missionaries, these exploiters frequently come as the "friend of the Negro," pretending to offer worthwhile goods and services, when their basic motivation is personal profit and

[5] Albert Sarraut, French Colonial Secretary of State, speaking at the Ecole Coloniale in Paris. As quoted in Kwame Nkrumah's *Africa Must Unite*. London: Heinemann Educational Books, Ltd., 1963, p. 40.

their basic impact is the maintenance of racism. Many of the social welfare agencies—public and private—frequently pretend to offer "uplift" services; in reality, they end up creating a system which dehumanizes the individual and perpetuates his dependency. Conscious or unconscious, the paternalistic attitude of many of these agencies is no different from that of many missionaries going into Africa.

Professor Kenneth Clark described the economic colonization of the *Dark Ghetto* as follows:

> The ghetto feeds upon itself; it does not produce goods or contribute to the prosperity of the city. It has few large businesses. . . . Even though the white community has tried to keep the Negro confined in ghetto pockets, the white businessman has not stayed out of the ghetto. A ghetto, too, offers opportunities for profit, and in a competitive society profit is to be made where it can.
>
> In Harlem there is only one large department store and that is owned by whites. Negroes own a savings and loan association; and one Negro-owned bank has recently been organized. The other banks are branches of white-owned downtown banks. Property—apartment houses, stores, businesses, bars, concessions, and theaters—are for the most part owned by persons who live outside the community and take their profits home. . . .
>
> When tumult arose in ghetto streets in the summer of 1964, most of the stores broken into and looted belonged to white men. Many of these owners responded to the destruction with bewilderment and anger, for they felt that they had been serving a community that needed them. *They did not realize* that the residents were not grateful for this service but bitter, as natives often feel toward the functionaries of a colonial power who in the very act of service, keep the hated *structure of oppression intact* [pp. 27–28].

It is a stark reality that the black communities are becoming more and more economically depressed. In June, 1966, the Bureau of Labor Statistics reported on the deteriorating condition of black people in this country. In 1948, the jobless rate of non-white [6] males between the ages of fourteen and nineteen was 7.6 percent. In 1965, the percentage of unemployment in this age group was 22.6 percent. The corresponding figures for unemployed white male teen-agers were 8.3 percent in 1948, and 11.8 percent in 1965.

In the ten-year period from 1955 to 1965, total employment for youth between the ages of fourteen and nineteen increased from 2,642,000 to 3,612,000. Non-white youth got only 36,000 of those 970,000 new jobs. As for adults, the ratio of non-white to white adult unemployment has remained double: in June, 1966, 4.1 percent for whites and 8.3 percent for non-whites.[7]

Lest someone talk about educational preparation, let it quickly be added here that *unemployment rates in 1965 were higher for non-white high school graduates than for white high school drop-outs.* Furthermore, the median income of a non-white male college graduate in 1960 was $5,020—actually $110 less than the earnings of white males with only one to three years of high school. Dr. Andrew F. Brimmer, the Negro former Assistant Secretary for Economic Affairs in the Department of Commerce, further highlights this situation in speaking of expected lifetime earnings:

> Perhaps the most striking feature . . . is the fact that a non-white man must have between one and three years of college before he can expect to earn as much as a white man with less than eight years of schooling, over the course of their respective working lives. *Moreover, even after completing college and spending at least one year in graduate*

[6] Non-white in this and subsequent statistics includes Puerto Ricans, but the vast majority of non-whites are black people.
[7] William A. Price, "Economics of the Negro Ghetto," *The National Guardian* (September 3, 1966), p. 4.

school, a non-white man can expect to do about as well as a
white person who only completed high school.[8]

A white man with four years of high school education can
expect to earn about $253,000 in his lifetime. A black man
with five years or more of college can expect to earn
$246,000 in his lifetime. Dr. Brimmer is presently a mem-
ber of the Federal Reserve Board, and many people will
point to his new position as an indication of "the progress
of Negroes." In Chapter II, we shall discuss the absurdity
of such conclusions.

Again, as in the African colonies, the black community
is sapped senseless of what economic resources it does have.
Through the exploitative system of credit, people pay "a
dollar down, a dollar a week" literally for years. Interest
rates are astronomical, and the merchandise—of relatively
poor quality in the first place—is long since worn out before
the final payment. Professor David Caplovitz of Columbia
University has commented in his book, *The Poor Pay
More*, "The high markup on low-quality goods is thus a
major device used by merchants to protect themselves
against the risks of their credit business" (p. 18). Many
of the ghetto citizens, because of unsteady employment
and low incomes, cannot obtain credit from more legitimate
businesses; thus they must do without important items or
end up being exploited. They are lured into the stores by
attractive advertising displays hawking, for example, three
rooms of furniture for "only $199." Once inside, the un-
suspecting customer is persuaded to buy lesser furniture at
a more expensive price, or he is told that the advertised
items are temporarily out of stock and is shown other goods.
More frequently than not, of course, all the items are over-
priced.

The exploitative merchant relies as much on threats as

[8] Andrew F. Brimmer, "The Negro in the National Economy," *The
American Negro Reference Book* (ed. by John P. Davis), Englewood Cliffs,
New Jersey: Prentice-Hall, 1966, p. 260.

he does on legal action to guarantee payment. Garnishment of wages is not particularly beneficial to the merchant—although certainly used—because the employer will frequently fire an employee rather than be subjected to the bother of extra bookkeeping. And once the buyer is fired, all payments stop. But the merchant can hold the threat of garnishment over the customer's head. Repossession is another threat; again, not particularly beneficial to the merchant. He knows the poor quality of his goods in the first place, and there is little resale value in such goods which have probably already received substantial use. In addition, both the methods of garnishment and repossession give the merchant a bad business image in the community. It is better business practice to raise the prices two to three hundred percent, get what he can—dogging the customer for that weekly payment—and still realize a sizeable profit. At the same time the merchant can protect his image as a "considerate, understanding fellow."

The merchant has special ways of victimizing public welfare recipients. They are not supposed to buy on credit; installment payments are not provided for in the budget. Thus a merchant can threaten to tell the caseworker if a recipient who isn't meeting his payments does not "come in and put down something, if only a couple of dollars." Another example: in November, 1966, M.E.N.D. (Massive Economic Neighborhood Development), a community action, anti-poverty agency in New York City, documented the fact that some merchants raise their prices on the days that welfare recipients receive their checks. Canned goods and other items were priced as much as ten cents more on those specific days.

Out of a substandard income, the black man pays exorbitant prices for cheap goods; he must then pay more for his housing than whites. Whitney Young, Jr. of the Urban League writes in his book, *To Be Equal:* "most of Chicago's 838,000 Negroes live in a ghetto and pay about

$20 more per month for housing than their white counter-parts in the city" (pp. 144–45). Black people also have a much more difficult time securing a mortgage. They must resort to real estate speculators who charge interest rates up to ten percent, whereas a FHA loan would carry only a six percent interest rate. As for loans to go into business, we find the same pattern as among Africans, who were pro-hibited or discouraged from starting commercial enter-prises. "The white power structure," says Dr. Clark in *Dark Ghetto*, "has collaborated in the economic serfdom of Negroes by its reluctance to give loans and insurance to Negro business" (pp. 27–28). The Small Business Ad-ministration, for example, in the ten-year period prior to 1964, made only *seven* loans to black people.

This is why the society does nothing meaningful about institutional racism: because the black community has been the creation of, and dominated by, a combination of oppressive forces and special interests in the white com-munity. The groups which have access to the necessary resources and the ability to effect change benefit politically and economically from the continued subordinate status of the black community. This is not to say that every single white American consciously oppresses black people. He does not need to. Institutional racism has been maintained de-liberately by the power structure and through indifference, inertia and lack courage on the part of white masses as well as petty officials. Whenever black demands for change become loud and strong, indifference is replaced by active opposition based on fear and self-interest. The line between purposeful suppression and indifference blurs. One way or another, most whites participate in economic colonialism.

Indeed, the colonial white power structure has been a most formidable foe. It has perpetuated a vicious circle—the poverty cycle—in which the black communities are denied good jobs, and therefore stuck with a low income and therefore unable to obtain a good education with which to obtain good jobs. (We shall discuss this in detail in Chapter VII.) They cannot qualify for credit at most reputable places; they then resort to unethical merchants who take advantage of them by charging higher prices for inferior goods. They end up having less funds to buy in bulk, thus unable to reduce overall costs. They remain trapped.

In the face of such realities, it becomes ludicrous to condemn black people for "not showing more initiative." Black people are not in a depressed condition because of some defect in their character. The colonial power structure clamped a boot of oppression on the neck of the black people and then, ironically, said "they are not ready for freedom." Left solely to the good will of the oppressor, the oppressed would never be ready.

And no one accepts blame. And there is no "white power structure" doing it to them. And they are in that condition "because they are lazy and don't want to work." And this is not colonialism. And this is the land of opportunity, and the home of the free. And people should not become alienated.

But people *do* become alienated.

■

The operation of political and economic colonialism in this country has had social repercussions which date back to slavery but did not by any means end with the Emancipation Proclamation. Perhaps the most vicious result of colonialism—in Africa and this country—was that it purposefully, maliciously and with reckless abandon relegated the black man to a subordinated, inferior status in the society. The individual was considered and treated as a lowly animal, not to be housed properly, or given adequate medical services, and by no means a decent education. In

Chapter VII we will discuss the specific effects of colonialism on the education, housing and health of black people; here, we shall concentrate on the human and psychological results of social colonialism, first as it affected white attitudes toward blacks and then the attitude of black people toward themselves.

As we have already noted, slaves were brought to this land for the good of white masters, not for the purpose of saving or "civilizing" the blacks. In *From Slavery to Freedom*, Professor John Hope Franklin writes:

> When the countries of Europe undertook to develop the New World, they were interested primarily in the exploitation of America's natural resources. Labor was, obviously, necessary, and the cheaper the better [p. 47].

Indians would have been a natural solution, but they were too susceptible to diseases carried by Europeans, and they would not conform to the rigid discipline of the plantation system. Poor whites of Europe were tried but proved unsatisfactory. They were only indentured servants, brought over to serve for a limited time; many refused to complete their contract and ran away. With their white skins, they assimilated easily enough into the society. But black Africans were different. They proved to be the white man's economic salvation. Franklin concludes:

> Because of their color, Negroes could be easily apprehended. Negroes could be purchased outright and a master's labor supply would not be in a state of constant fluctuation. Negroes, from a pagan land and without exposure to the ethical ideals of Christianity, could be handled with more rigid methods of discipline and could be morally and spiritually degraded for the sake of stability on the plantation. In the long run, Negro slaves were actually cheaper. In a period when economic considerations were so vital, this was especially important. Negro slavery, then, became a fixed institution, a solution to one of the most difficult problems that arose in the New World. With the supply of Negroes appar-

ently inexhaustible, there would be no more worries about labor. European countries could look back with gratitude to the first of their nationals who explored the coasts of Africa, and brought back gold to Europe. It was the key to the solution of one of America's most pressing problems [p. 49].

The fact of slavery had to have profound impact on the subsequent attitudes of the larger society toward the black man. The fact of slavery helped to fix the sense of superior group position. Chief Justice Taney, in the Dred Scott decision of 1857, stated ". . . that they (black people) had no rights which the white man was bound to respect; and that the negro might justly and lawfully be reduced to slavery for his benefit." The emancipation of the slaves by legal act could certainly not erase such notions from the minds of racists. They believed in their superior status, not in paper documents. And that belief has persisted. When some people compare the black American to "other immigrant" groups in this country, they overlook the fact that slavery was peculiar to the blacks. No other minority group in this country was ever treated as legal property.

Even when the black man has participated in wars to defend this country, even when the black man has repeatedly demonstrated loyalty to this country, the embedded colonial mentality has continued to deny him equal status in the social order. Participation of black men in the white man's wars is a characteristic of colonialism. The colonial ruler readily calls upon and expects the subjects to fight and die in defense of the colonial empire, without the ruler feeling any particular compulsion to grant the subjects equal status. In fact, the war is frequently one to defend the socio-political status quo established between the ruler and subject. Whatever else may be changed by wars, the fundamental relation between colonial master and subordinates remains substantially unaltered.

Woodrow Wilson proclaimed that this country entered World War I "to make the world safe for democracy."

This was the very same President who issued executive orders segregating most of the eating and rest-room facilities for federal employees. This was the same man who had written in 1901:

> An extraordinary and very perilous state of affairs had been created in the South by the sudden and absolute emancipation of the Negroes, and it was not strange that the Southern legislatures should deem it necessary to take extraordinary steps to guard against the manifest and pressing dangers which it entailed. Here was a vast "laboring, landless, homeless class," once slaves; now free; unpracticed in liberty, unschooled in self-control; never sobered by the discipline of self-support; never established in any habit of prudence; excited by a freedom they did not understand, exalted by false hopes, bewildered and without leaders, and yet insolent and aggressive; sick of work, covetous of pleasure—a host of dusky children untimely put out of school.[9]

". . . dusky children untimely put out of school," freed too soon—it is absolutely inconceivable that a man who spoke in such a manner could have black people in mind when he talked of saving the world (i.e., the United States) for democracy. Obviously, black people were not included in Woodrow Wilson's defense perimeter. Whatever the life of blacks might have been under German rule, this country clearly did not fight Germany for the improvement of the status of black people—under the saved democracy—in *this* land.

Even during the war, while black soldiers were dying in Europe, Representative Frank Park of Georgia introduced a bill to make it unlawful to appoint blacks to the rank of either noncommissioned or commissioned officers. Following the war, black veterans returned to face a struggle no less fierce than the one overseas. More than seventy black people were lynched during the first year after armis-

[9] Woodrow Wilson, "Reconstruction in the Southern States," *Atlantic Monthly* (January, 1901).

tice. Ten black soldiers, some still in uniform, were lynched. And few who are knowledgeable of twentieth-century American history will fail to remember "the Red summer" of 1919. Twenty-five race riots were recorded between June and December of that year. The Ku Klux Klan flourished during this period, making more than two hundred public appearances in twenty-seven states. The Klan cells were not all located in the South; units were organized in New York, Indiana, Illinois, Michigan and other northern cities.

World War II was basically little different. The increased need for manpower in defense industries slowly opened up more jobs for black people as a result of the war effort, but as Professor Garfinkel has pointed out in *When Negroes March*, "When defense jobs were finally opened up to Negroes, they tended to be on the lowest rungs of the success ladder." Garfinkel also tells of how the President of the North American Aviation Company, for example, issued this statement on May 7, 1941:

> While we are in complete sympathy with the Negroes, it is against company policy to employ them as aircraft workers or mechanics . . . regardless of their training. . . . There will be some jobs as janitors for Negroes [p. 17].

This country also saw fit to treat German prisoners of war more humanely than it treated its own black soldiers. On one occasion, a group of black soldiers was transporting German prisoners by train through the South to a prisoner-of-war camp. The railroad diner required the black American soldiers to eat in segregated facilities on the train—only four at a time and with considerable delay—while the German prisoners (white, of course) ate without delay and with other passengers in the main section of the diner!

Thus does white man regard the black, an attitude rooted in slavery. Clearly it would be and has been very difficult for subsequent generations of whites to overcome—even if they wanted to—the concept of a subordinate caste assigned

to blacks, of black inferiority. They had to continue thinking this way and developing elaborate doctrines to justify
what Professor Williams has called "the inevitability and
rightness of the existing scheme of things." Herbert Blumer
draws the following conclusion:

> . . . The sense of group position is a norm and imperative—
> indeed, a very powerful one. It guides, incites, cows, and
> coerces . . . this kind of sense of group position stands for
> and involves a fundamental kind of group affiliation for the
> members of the dominant racial group. To the extent that
> they recognize themselves as belonging to that group they
> will automatically come under the influence of the sense of
> position held by that group.[10]

Blumer allows for the exception: those who do not
recognize themselves as belonging to the group. Inside and
outside the civil rights movement, there have been whites
who rejected their own whiteness as a group symbol and
who even tried sometimes "to be black." These dissidents
have endured ostracism, poverty, physical pain and death
itself in demonstrating their non-recognition of belonging
to the group because of its racism. But how fully can white
people free themselves from the tug of the group position—
free themselves not so much from overt racist attitudes in
themselves as from a more subtle paternalism bred into
them by the society and, perhaps more important, from
the conditioned reaction of black people to their whiteness? For most whites, that freedom is unattainable. White
civil rights workers themselves have often noted this:

> Too often we have found our relationships with the local
> community leaders disturbingly like the traditional white-
> black relationship of the deep South: the white organizer
> finds the decision-making left up to him, while the local
> leader finds himself instinctively assuming a subservient

[10] Herbert Blumer, "Race Prejudice as a Sense of Group Positions,"
Pacific Sociological Review (Spring, 1958).

role. . . . Since the organizer's purpose is not to lead but to get the people to lead themselves, being white is an unsurmountable handicap.[11]

The social and psychological effects on black people of all their degrading experiences are also very clear. From the time black people were introduced into this country, their condition has fostered human indignity and the denial of respect. Born into this society today, black people begin to doubt themselves, their worth as human beings. Self-respect becomes almost impossible. Kenneth Clark describes the process in *Dark Ghetto*:

> Human beings who are forced to live under ghetto conditions and whose daily experience tells them that almost nowhere in society are they respected and granted the ordinary dignity and courtesy accorded to others will, as a matter of course, begin to doubt their own worth. Since every human being depends upon his cumulative experiences with others for clues as to how he should view and value himself, children who are consistently rejected understandably begin to question and doubt whether they, their family, and their group really deserve no more respect from the larger society than they receive. These doubts become the seeds of a pernicious self- and group-hatred, the Negro's complex and debilitating prejudice against himself.
>
> The preoccupation of many Negroes with hair straighteners, skin bleachers, and the like illustrates this tragic aspect of American racial prejudice—Negroes have come to believe in their own inferiority [pp. 63–64].

There was the same result in Africa. And some European colonial powers—notably France and Portugal—provided the black man "a way out" of the degrading status: to become "white," or assimilated. France pursued a colonial policy aimed at producing a black French elite class, a group exposed and acculturated to French "civilization."

[11] Bruce Detwiler, "A Time to be Black," *The New Republic* (September 17, 1966).

In its African colonies of Mozambique and Angola, Portugal has attempted a colonial policy of assimilation which goes even further. There is no pretense—as in the British colonies and in American rhetoric—of black people moving toward self-government and freedom. All Independence groups have been suppressed. There prevails in these Portuguese colonies a legal process whereby an African may become, in effect, a "white" man if he measures up to certain Western standards. The *assimilado* is one who has adopted Portuguese customs, dress, language, and has achieved at least a high school education. He is, of course, favored with special jobs and better housing. This status likewise qualifies him to receive a passport to travel abroad, mainly to Portugal and Brazil. Otherwise, such freedom of movement is denied. The *assimilado* is accepted socially by the whites in the restaurants and night clubs. In fact, the Portuguese officials will even import a white Portuguese woman to Mozambique to marry an *assimilado* man. (American colonialism has not gone this far.) But to submit to all of this, the *assimilado* must reject as intrinsically inferior his entire African heritage and association.

In a manner similar to that of the colonial powers in Africa, American society indicates avenues of escape from the ghetto for those individuals who adapt to the "mainstream." This adaptation means to disassociate oneself from the black race, its culture, community and heritage, and become immersed (dispersed is another term) in the white world. What actually happens, as Professor E. Franklin Frazier pointed out in his book, *Black Bourgeoisie*, is that the black person ceases to identify himself with black people yet is obviously unable to assimilate with whites. He becomes a "marginal man," living on the fringes of both societies in a world largely of "make believe." This black person is urged to adopt American middle-class standards and values. As with the black African who had to become a

"Frenchman" in order to be accepted, so to be an American, the black man must strive to become "white." To the extent that he does, he is considered "well adjusted"—one who has "risen above the race question." These people are frequently held up by the white Establishment as living examples of the progress being made by the society in solving the race problem. Suffice it to say that precisely because they are required to denounce—overtly or covertly —their black race, *they are reinforcing racism in this country.*

In the United States, as in Africa, their "adaptation" operated to deprive the black community of its potential skills and brain power. All too frequently, these "integrated" people are used to blunt the true feelings and goals of the black masses. They are picked as "Negro leaders," and the white power structure proceeds to talk to and deal only with them. Needless to say, no fruitful, meaningful dialogue can take place under such circumstances. Those hand-picked "leaders" have no viable constituency for which they can speak and act. All this is a classic formula of colonial co-optation.

At all times, then, the social effects of colonialism are to degrade and to dehumanize the subjected black man. White America's School of Slavery and Segregation, like the School of Colonialism, has taught the subject to hate himself and to deny his own humanity. The white society maintains an attitude of superiority and the black community has too often succumbed to it, thereby permitting the whites to believe in the correctness of their position. Racist assumptions of white superiority have been so deeply engrained into the fiber of the society that they infuse the entire functioning of the national subconscious. They are taken for granted and frequently not even recognized. As Professors Lewis Killian and Charles Grigg express it in their book, *Racial Crisis in America:*

At the present time, integration as a solution to the race problem demands that the Negro foreswear his identity as a Negro. But for a lasting solution, the meaning of "American" must lose its implicit racial modifier, "white." Even without biological amalgamation, integration requires a sincere acceptance by all Americans that it is just as good to be a black American as to be a white American. Here is the crux of the problem of race relations—the redefinition of the sense of group position so that the status advantage of the white man is no longer an advantage, so that an American may acknowledge his Negro ancestry without apologizing for it. . . . They [black people] live in a society in which to be unconditionally "American" is to be white, and to be black is a misfortune [pp. 108–9].

The time is long overdue for the black community to redefine itself, set forth new values and goals, and organize around them.

BLACK POWER:

◑ "To carve out a place for itself in the politico-social order," V. O. Key, Jr. wrote in *Politics, Parties and Pressure Groups*, " a new group may have to fight for reorientation of many of the values of the old order" (p. 57). This is especially true when that group is composed of black people in the American society—a society that has for centuries deliberately and systematically excluded them from political participation. Black people in the United States must raise hard questions, questions which challenge the very nature of the society itself: its long-standing values, beliefs and institutions.

To do this, we must first redefine ourselves. Our basic need is to reclaim our history and our identity from what

Its Need and Substance

must be called cultural terrorism, from the depredation of self-justifying white guilt. We shall have to struggle for the right to create our own terms through which to define ourselves and our relationship to the society, and to have these terms recognized. This is the first necessity of a free people, and the first right that any oppressor must suspend.

In *Politics Among Nations*, Hans Morgenthau defined political power as "the psychological control over the minds of men" (p. 29). This control includes the attempt by the oppressor to have *his* definitions, *his* historical descriptions, *accepted* by the oppressed. This was true in Africa no less than in the United States. To black Africans, the word "Uhuru" means "freedom," but they had to fight the white colonizers for the right to use the term. The recorded history of this country's dealings with red and black men offers other examples. In the wars between the white settlers and the "Indians," a battle won by the Cavalry was described as a "victory." The "Indians'" triumphs, however, were "massacres." (The American colonists were not unaware of the need to define their acts in their own terms. They labeled their fight against England a "revolution"; the English attempted to demean it by calling it "insubordination" or "riotous.")

The historical period following Reconstruction in the South after the Civil War has been called by many historians the period of Redemption, implying that the bigoted southern slave societies were "redeemed" from the hands of "reckless and irresponsible" black rulers. Professor John Hope Franklin's *Reconstruction* or Dr. W. E. B. Dubois' *Black Reconstruction* should be sufficient to dispel inaccurate historical notions, but the larger society persists in its own self-serving accounts. Thus black people came to be depicted as "lazy," "apathetic," "dumb," "shiftless," "good-timers." Just as red men had to be recorded as "savages" to justify the white man's theft of their land, so black men had to be vilified in order to justify their continued oppression. Those who have the right to define are the masters of the situation. Lewis Carroll understood this:

> "When I use a word," Humpty Dumpty said in a rather scornful tone, "it means just what I choose it to mean— neither more nor less."
> "The question is," said Alice, "whether you *can* make words mean so many different things."
> "The question is," said Humpty Dumpty, "which is to be master—that's all." *

* Lewis Carroll, *Through the Looking Glass*. New York: Doubleday Books, Inc., p. 196.

Today, the American educational system continues to reinforce the entrenched values of the society through the
use of words. Few people in this country question that this
is "the land of the free and the home of the brave." They
have had these words drummed into them from childhood.
Few people question that this is the "Great Society" or
that this country is fighting "Communist aggression"
around the world. We mouth these things over and over,
and they become truisms not to be questioned. In a similar
way, black people have been saddled with epithets.

"Integration" is another current example of a word which
has been defined according to the way white Americans see
it. To many of them, it means black men wanting to marry
white daughters; it means "race mixing"—implying bed or
dance partners. To black people, it has meant a way to improve their lives—economically and politically. But the pre-
dominant white definition has stuck in the minds of too
many people.

Black people must redefine themselves, and only *they* can
do that. Throughout this country, vast segments of the
black communities are beginning to recognize the need
to assert their own definitions, to reclaim their history,
their culture; to create their own sense of community and
togetherness. There is a growing resentment of the word
"Negro," for example, because this term is the invention
of our oppressor; it is *his* image of us that he describes.
Many blacks are now calling themselves African-Americans,
Afro-Americans or black people because that is *our* image
of ourselves. When we begin to define our own image, the
stereotypes—that is, lies—that our oppressor has developed
will begin in the white community and end there. The
black community will have a positive image of itself that *it*
has created. This means we will no longer call ourselves
lazy, apathetic, dumb, good-timers, shiftless, etc. Those are
words used by white America to define us. If we accept
these adjectives, as some of us have in the past, then we

see ourselves only in a negative way, precisely the way white America wants us to see ourselves. Our incentive is broken and our will to fight is surrendered. From now on we shall view ourselves as African-Americans and as black people who are in fact energetic, determined, intelligent, beautiful and peace-loving.

There is a terminology and ethos peculiar to the black community of which black people are beginning to be no longer ashamed. Black communities are the only large segments of this society where people refer to each other as brother—soul-brother, soul-sister. Some people may look upon this as *ersatz*, as make-believe, but it is not that. It is real. It is a growing sense of community. It is a growing realization that black Americans have a common bond not only among themselves, but with their African brothers. In *Black Man's Burden*, John O. Killens described his trip to ten African countries as follows:

> Everywhere I went people called me brother. . . . "Welcome, American brother." It was a good feeling for me, to be in Africa. To walk in a land for the first time in your entire life knowing within yourself that your color would not be held against you. No black man ever knows this in America [p. 160].

More and more black Americans are developing this feeling. They are becoming aware that they have a history which pre-dates their forced introduction to this country. African-American history means a long history beginning on the continent of Africa, a history not taught in the standard textbooks of this country. It is absolutely essential that black people know this history, that they know their roots, that they develop an awareness of their cultural heritage. Too long have they been kept in submission by being told that they had no culture, no manifest heritage, before they landed on the slave auction blocks in this country. If black people are to know themselves as a vibrant, valiant people, they must know their roots. And they will soon learn that the Hollywood image of man-eating cannibals waiting for, and waiting on, the Great White Hunter is a lie.

With redefinition will come a clearer notion of the role black Americans can play in this world. This role will emerge clearly out of the unique, common experiences of Afro-Asians. Killens concludes:

> I believe furthermore that the American Negro can be the bridge between the West and Africa-Asia. We black Americans can serve as a bridge to mutual understanding. The one thing we black Americans have in common with the other colored peoples of the world is that we have all felt the cruel and ruthless heel of white supremacy. We have all been "niggerized" on one level or another. And all of us are determined to "deniggerize" the earth. To rid the world of "niggers" is the Black Man's Burden, human reconstruction is the grand objective [p. 176].

Only when black people fully develop this sense of community, of themselves, can they begin to deal effectively with the problems of racism in *this* country. This is what we mean by a new consciousness; this is the vital first step.

■

The next step is what we shall call the process of political modernization—a process which must take place if the society is to be rid of racism. "Political modernization" includes many things, but we mean by it three major concepts: (1) questioning old values and institutions of the society; (2) searching for new and different forms of political structure to solve political and economic problems; and (3) broadening the base of political participation to include more people in the decision-making process. These notions (we shall take up each in turn) are central to our thinking throughout this book and to contemporary American history as a whole. As David Apter wrote in

The Politics of Modernization, ". . . the struggle to modernize is what has given meaning to our generation. It tests our cherished institutions and our beliefs. . . . So compelling a force has it become that we are forced to ask new questions of our own institutions. Each country, whether modernized or modernizing, stands in both judgment and fear of the results. Our own society is no exception" (p. 2).

The values of this society support a racist system; we find it incongruous to ask black people to adopt and support most of those values. We also reject the assumption that the basic institutions of this society must be preserved. The goal of black people must *not* be to assimilate into middle-class America, for that class—as a whole—is without a viable conscience as regards humanity. The values of the middle class permit the perpetuation of the ravages of the black community. The values of that class are based on material aggrandizement, not the expansion of humanity. The values of that class ultimately support cloistered little closed societies tucked away neatly in tree-lined suburbia. The values of that class do *not* lead to the creation of an open society. That class *mouths* its preference for a free, competitive society, while at the same time forcefully and even viciously denying to black people as a group the opportunity to compete.

We are not unmindful of other descriptions of the social utility of the middle class. Banfield and Wilson, in *City Politics,* concluded:

> The departure of the middle class from the central city is important in other ways. . . . The middle class supplies a social and political leavening in the life of a city. Middle-class people demand good schools and integrity in government. They support churches, lodges, parent-teacher associations, scout troops, better-housing committees, art galleries, and operas. It is the middle class, in short, that asserts a conception of the public interest. Now its activity is increasingly concentrated in the suburbs [p. 14].

But this same middle class manifests a sense of superior group position in regard to race. This class wants "good government" *for themselves;* it wants good schools *for its children.* At the same time, many of its members sneak into the black community by day, exploit it, and take the money home to their middle-class communities at night to support their operas and art galleries and comfortable homes. When not actually robbing, they will fight off the handful of more affluent black people who seek to move in; when they approve or even seek token integration, it applies only to black people like themselves—as "white" as possible. *This class is the backbone of institutional racism in this country.*

Thus we reject the goal of assimilation into middle-class America because the values of that class are in themselves anti-humanist and because that class as a social force perpetuates racism. We must face the fact that, in the past, what we have called the movement has not really questioned the middle-class values and institutions of this country. If anything, it has accepted those values and institutions without fully realizing their racist nature. Re-orientation means an emphasis on the dignity of man, not on the sanctity of property. It means the creation of a society where human misery and poverty are repugnant to that society, not an indication of laziness or lack of initiative. The creation of new values means the establishment of a society based, as Killens expresses it in *Black Man's Burden,* on "free people," not "free enterprise" (p. 167). To do this means to modernize—*indeed, to civilize*—this country.

Supporting the old values are old political and economic structures; these must also be "modernized." We should at this point distinguish between "structures" and "system." By system, we have in mind the entire American complex of basic institutions, values, beliefs, etc. By structures, we mean the specific institutions (political parties, interest groups, bureaucratic administrations) which exist to conduct the business of that system. Obviously, the first is broader than the second. Also, the second assumes the legitimacy of the first. Our view is that, given the illegitimacy of the system, we cannot then proceed to transform that system with existing structures.

The two major political parties in this country have become non-viable entities for the legitimate representation of the real needs of masses—especially blacks—in this country. Walter Lippmann raised the same point in his syndicated column of December 8, 1966. He pointed out that the party system in the United States developed before our society became as technologically complex as it is now. He says that the ways in which men live and define themselves are changing radically. Old ideological issues, once the subject of passionate controversy, Lippmann argues, are of little interest today. He asks whether the great urban complexes—which are rapidly becoming the centers of black population in the U.S.—can be run with the same systems and ideas that derive from a time when America was a country of small villages and farms. While not addressing himself directly to the question of race, Lippmann raises a major question about our political institutions; and the crisis of race in America may be its major symptom.

Black people have seen the city planning commissions, the urban renewal commissions, the boards of education and the police departments fail to speak to their needs in a meaningful way. We must devise new structures, new institutions to replace those forms or to make them responsive. There is nothing sacred or inevitable about old institutions; the focus must be on people, not forms.

Existing structures and established ways of doing things have a way of perpetuating themselves and for this reason, the modernizing process will be difficult. Therefore, timidity in calling into question the boards of education or the police departments will not do. They must be challenged forcefully and clearly. If this means the creation of parallel community institutions, then that must be the solution. If this means that black parents must gain control over the operation of the schools in the black community, then that must be the solution. The search for new forms means the search for institutions that will, for once, make decisions in the interest of black people. It means, for example, a building inspection department that neither winks at violations of building codes by absentee slumlords nor imposes meaningless fines which permit them to continue their exploitation of the black community.

Essential to the modernization of structures is a broadened base of political participation. More and more people must become politically sensitive and active (we have already seen this happening in some areas of the South). People must no longer be tied, by small incentives or handouts, to a corrupting and corruptible white machine. Black people will choose their own leaders and hold those leaders responsible to *them*. A broadened base means an end to the condition described by James Wilson in *Negro Politics*, whereby "Negroes tended to be the objects rather than the subjects of civic action. Things are often done for, or about, or to, or because of Negroes, but they are less frequently done *by* Negroes" (p. 133). Broadening the base of political participation, then, has as much to do with the quality of black participation as with the quantity. We are fully aware that the black vote, especially in the North, has been pulled out of white pockets and "delivered" whenever it was in the interest of white politicians to do so. That vote must no longer be controllable by those who have neither the interests nor the demonstrated concern of black people in mind.

As the base broadens, as more and more black people become activated, they will perceive more clearly the special disadvantages heaped upon them as a group. They will perceive that the larger society is growing more affluent while the black society is retrogressing, as daily life and mounting statistics clearly show (see Chapters I and VIII). V. O. Key describes what often happens next, in *Politics, Parties and Pressure Groups:* "A factor of great significance in the setting off of political movements is an abrupt change for the worse in the status of one group relative to that of other groups in society. . . . A rapid change for the worse . . . in the relative status of any group . . . is likely to precipitate political action" (p. 24). Black people will become increasingly active as they notice that their retrogressive status exists in large measure because of values and institutions arraigned against them. They will begin to stress and strain and call the entire system into question. Political modernization will be in motion. We believe that it is now in motion. One form of that motion is Black Power.

■

The adoption of the concept of Black Power is one of the most legitimate and healthy developments in American politics and race relations in our time. The concept of Black Power speaks to all the needs mentioned in this chapter. It is a call for black people in this country to unite, to recognize their heritage, to build a sense of community. It is a call for black people to begin to define their own goals, to lead their own organizations and to support those organizations. It is a call to reject the racist institutions and values of this society.

The concept of Black Power rests on a fundamental premise: *Before a group can enter the open society, it must first close ranks.* By this we mean that group solidarity is necessary before a group can operate effectively from a bargaining position of strength in a pluralistic society. Traditionally, each new ethnic group in this society has found the route to social and political viability through the organization of its own institutions with which to represent its needs within the larger society. Studies in voting behavior specifically, and political behavior generally, have made it clear that politically the American pot has not melted. Italians vote for Rubino over O'Brien; Irish for Murphy over Goldberg, etc. This phenomenon may seem distasteful to some, but it has been and remains today a central fact of the American political system. There are other examples of ways in which groups in the society have remembered their roots and used this effectively in the political arena. Theodore Sorensen describes the politics of foreign aid during the Kennedy Administration in his book *Kennedy:*

> No powerful constituencies or interest groups backed foreign aid. The Marshall Plan at least had appealed to Americans who traced their roots to the Western European nations aided. But there were few voters who identified with India, Colombia or Tanganyika [p. 351].

The extent to which black Americans can and do "trace their roots" to Africa, to that extent will they be able to be more effective on the political scene.

A white reporter set forth this point in other terms when he made the following observation about white Mississippi's manipulation of the anti-poverty program:

> The war on poverty has been predicated on the notion that there is such a thing as a community which can be defined geographically and mobilized for a collective effort to help the poor. This theory has no relationship to reality in the deep South. In every Mississippi county there are two communities. Despite all the pious platitudes of the moderates on both sides, these two communities habitually see their interests in terms of conflict rather than cooperation. Only when the Negro community can muster enough political, economic and professional strength to compete on somewhat equal terms, will Negroes believe in the possibility of true cooperation and whites accept its necessity. En route to integration, the Negro community needs to develop a greater independence—a chance to run its own affairs and not cave in whenever "the man" barks—or so it seems to me, and to

most of the knowledgeable people with whom I talked in
Mississippi. To OEO, this judgment may sound like black
nationalism. . . .[1]

The point is obvious: black people must lead and run
their own organizations. Only black people can convey the
revolutionary idea—and it is a revolutionary idea—that black
people are able to do things themselves. Only they can help
create in the community an aroused and continuing black
consciousness that will provide the basis for political
strength. In the past, white allies have often furthered white
supremacy without the whites involved realizing it, or even
wanting to do so. Black people must come together and do
things for themselves. They must achieve self-identity and
self-determination in order to have their daily needs met.

Black Power means, for example, that in Lowndes
County, Alabama, a black sheriff can end police brutality.
A black tax assessor and tax collector and county board of
revenue can lay, collect, and channel tax monies for the
building of better roads and schools serving black people.
In such areas as Lowndes, where black people have a majority, they will attempt to use power to exercise control.
This is what they seek: control. When black people lack a
majority, Black Power means proper representation and
sharing of control. It means the creation of power bases,
of strength, from which black people can press to change
local or nation-wide patterns of oppression—instead of from
weakness.

It does not mean *merely* putting black faces into office.
Black visibility is not Black Power. Most of the black politicians around the country today are not examples of Black
Power. The power must be that of a community, and ema-
nate from there. The black politicians must start from
there. The black politicians must stop being representatives

---

[1] Christopher Jencks, "Accommodating Whites: A New Look at Mississippi," *The New Republic* (April 16, 1966).

of "downtown" machines, whatever the cost might be in terms of lost patronage and holiday handouts.

Black Power recognizes—it must recognize—the ethnic basis of American politics as well as the power-oriented nature of American politics. Black Power therefore calls for black people to consolidate behind their own, so that they can bargain from a position of strength. But while we endorse the *procedure* of group solidarity and identity for the purpose of attaining certain goals in the body politic, this does not mean that black people should strive for the same kind of rewards (i.e., end results) obtained by the white society. The ultimate values and goals are not domination or exploitation of other groups, but rather an effective share in the total power of the society.

Nevertheless, some observers have labeled those who advocate Black Power as racists; they have said that the call for self-identification and self-determination is "racism in reverse" or "black supremacy." This is a deliberate and absurd lie. There is no analogy—by any stretch of definition or imagination—between the advocates of Black Power and white racists. Racism is not merely exclusion on the basis of race but exclusion for the purpose of subjugating or maintaining subjugation. The goal of the racists is to keep black people on the bottom, arbitrarily and dictatorially, as they have done in this country for over three hundred years. The goal of black self-determination and black self-identity—Black Power—is full participation in the decision-making processes affecting the lives of black people, and recognition of the virtues in themselves as black people. The black people of this country have not lynched whites, bombed their churches, murdered their children and manipulated laws and institutions to maintain oppression. White racists have. Congressional laws, one after the other, have not been necessary to stop black people from oppressing others and denying others the full enjoyment of their rights. White racists have made such laws necessary. The goal of Black Power is positive and functional to a free and viable society. No white racist can make this claim.

A great deal of public attention and press space was devoted to the hysterical accusation of "black racism" when the call for Black Power was first sounded. A national committee of influential black churchmen affiliated with the National Council of Churches, despite their obvious respectability and responsibility, had to resort to a paid advertisement to articulate their position, while anyone yapping "black racism" made front-page news. In their statement, published in the *New York Times* of July 31, 1966, the churchmen said:

> We, an informal group of Negro churchmen in America, are deeply disturbed about the crisis brought upon our country by historic distortions of important human realities in the controversy about "black power." What we see shining through the variety of rhetoric is not anything new but the same old problem of power and race which has faced our beloved country since 1619.
>
> . . . The conscience of black men is corrupted because having no power to implement the demands of conscience, the concern for justice in the absence of justice becomes a chaotic self-surrender. Powerlessness breeds a race of beggars. We are faced with a situation where powerless conscience meets conscienceless power, threatening the very foundations of our Nation.
>
> We deplore the overt violence of riots, but we feel it is more important to focus on the real sources of these eruptions. These sources may be abetted inside the Ghetto, but their basic cause lies in the silent and covert violence which white middle class America inflicts upon the victims of the inner city.
>
> . . . In short, the failure of American leaders to use American power to create equal opportunity *in life* as well as *law*, this is the real problem and not the anguished cry for black power.
>
> . . . Without the capacity to participate with power, i.e.,

to have some organized political and economic strength to really influence people with whom one interacts, integration is not meaningful.

. . . America has asked its Negro citizens to fight for opportunity as *individuals*, whereas at certain points in our history what we have needed most has been opportunity for the *whole group*, not just for selected and approved Negroes.

. . . We must not apologize for the existence of this form of group power, for we have been oppressed as a group and not as individuals. We will not find our way out of that oppression until both we and America accept the need for Negro Americans, as well as for Jews, Italians, Poles, and white Anglo-Saxon Protestants, among others, to have and to wield group power.

It is a commentary on the fundamentally racist nature of this society that the concept of group strength for black people must be articulated—not to mention defended. No other group would submit to being led by others. Italians do not run the Anti-Defamation League of B'nai B'rith. Irish do not chair Christopher Columbus Societies. Yet when black people call for black-run and all-black organizations, they are immediately classed in a category with the Ku Klux Klan. This is interesting and ironic, but by no means surprising: the society does not expect black people to be able to take care of their business, and there are many who prefer it precisely that way.

In the end, we cannot and shall not offer any guarantees that Black Power, if achieved, would be non-racist. No one can predict human behavior. Social change always has unanticipated consequences. If black racism is what the larger society fears, we cannot help them. We can only state what we hope will be the result, given the fact that the present situation is unacceptable and that we have no real alternative but to work for Black Power. The final truth is that the white society is not entitled to reassurances, even if it were possible to offer them.

We have outlined the meaning and goals of Black Power; we have also discussed one major thing which it is not. There are others of greater importance. The advocates of Black Power reject the old slogans and meaningless rhetoric of previous years in the civil rights struggle. The language of yesterday is indeed irrelevant: progress, non-violence, integration, fear of "white backlash," coalition. Let us look at the rhetoric and see why these terms must be set aside or redefined.

One of the tragedies of the struggle against racism is that up to this point there has been no national organization which could speak to the growing militancy of young black people in the urban ghettos and the black-belt South. There has been only a "civil rights" movement, whose tone of voice was adapted to an audience of middle-class whites. It served as a sort of buffer zone between that audience and angry young blacks. It claimed to speak for the needs of a community, but it did not speak in the tone of that community. None of its so-called leaders could go into a rioting community and be listened to. In a sense, the blame must be shared—along with the mass media—by those leaders for what happened in Watts, Harlem, Chicago, Cleveland and other places. Each time the black people in those cities saw Dr. Martin Luther King get slapped they became angry. When they saw little black girls bombed to death *in a church* and civil rights workers ambushed and murdered, they were angrier; and when nothing happened, they were steaming mad. We had nothing to offer that they could see, except to go out and be beaten again. We helped to build their frustration.

We had only the old language of love and suffering. And in most places—that is, from the liberals and middle class—we got back the old language of patience and progress. The civil rights leaders were saying to the country: "Look, you guys are supposed to be nice guys, and we are only going to do what we are supposed to do. Why do you beat us up? Why don't you give us what we ask? Why don't you straighten yourselves out?" For the masses of black people, this language resulted in virtually nothing. In fact, their objective day-to-day condition worsened. The unemployment rate among black people increased while that among whites declined. Housing conditions in the black communities deteriorated. Schools in the black ghettos continued to plod along on outmoded techniques, inadequate curricula, and with all too many tired and indifferent teachers. Meanwhile, the President picked up the refrain of "We Shall Overcome" while the Congress passed civil rights law after civil rights law, only to have them effectively nullified by deliberately weak enforcement. "Progress is being made," we were told.

Such language, along with admonitions to remain non-violent and fear the white backlash, convinced some that that course was the *only* course to follow. It misled some into believing that a black minority could bow its head and get whipped into a meaningful position of power. The very notion is absurd. The white society devised the language, adopted the rules and had the black community narcotized into believing that that language and those rules were, in fact, relevant. The black community was told time and again how *other* immigrants finally won *acceptance:* that is, by following the Protestant Ethic of Work and Achievement. They worked hard; therefore, they achieved. We were not told that it was by building Irish Power, Italian Power, Polish Power or Jewish Power that these groups got themselves together and operated from positions of strength. We were not told that "the American dream" wasn't designed for black people. That while to-day, to whites, the dream may *seem* to include black people, it cannot do so by the very nature of this nation's political and economic system, which imposes institutional racism on the black masses if not upon every individual black. A notable comment on that "dream" was made by

Dr. Percy Julian, the black scientist and director of the Julian Research Institute in Chicago, a man for whom the dream seems to have come true. While not subscribing to "black power" as he understood it, Dr. Julian clearly understood the basis for it: "The false concept of basic Negro inferiority is one of the curses that still lingers. It is a problem created by the white man. Our children just no longer are going to accept the patience we were taught by our generation. We were taught a pretty little lie—excel and the whole world lies open before you. *I obeyed the injunction and found it to be wishful thinking.*" (Authors' italics) [2]

A key phrase in our buffer-zone days was <u>non-violence.</u> For years it has been thought that black people would not literally fight for their lives. Why this has been so is not entirely clear; neither the larger society nor black people are noted for passivity. The notion apparently stems from the years of marches and demonstrations and sit-ins where black people did not strike back and the violence always came from white mobs. There are many who still sincerely believe in that approach. From our viewpoint, rampaging white mobs and white night-riders must be made to understand that their days of free head-whipping are over. Black people should and must fight back. Nothing more quickly repels someone bent on destroying you than the unequivocal message: "O.K., fool, make your move, and run the same risk I run—of dying."

When the concept of Black Power is set forth, many people immediately conjure up notions of violence. The country's reaction to the Deacons for Defense and Justice, which originated in Louisiana, is instructive. Here is a group which realized that the "law" and law enforcement agencies would not protect people, so they had to do it themselves. If a nation fails to protect its citizens, then that nation cannot condemn those who take up the task them-

[2] *The New York Times* (April 30, 1967), p. 30.

selves. The Deacons and all other blacks who resort to self-defense represent a simple answer to a simple question: what man would not defend his family and home from attack?

But this frightened some white people, because they knew that black people would now fight back. They knew that this was precisely what *they* would have long since done if *they* were subjected to the injustices and oppression heaped on blacks. Those of us who advocate Black Power are quite clear in our own minds that a "non-violent" approach to civil rights is an approach black people cannot afford and a luxury white people do not deserve. It is crystal clear to us—and it must become so with the white society —*that there can be no social order without social justice*. White people must be made to understand that they must stop messing with black people, or the blacks *will* fight back!

Next, we must deal with the term "integration." According to its advocates, social justice will be accomplished by "integrating the Negro into the mainstream institutions of the society from which he has been traditionally excluded." This concept is based on the assumption that there is nothing of value in the black community and that little of value could be created among black people. The thing to do is siphon off the "acceptable" black people into the surrounding middle-class white community.

The goals of integrationists are middle-class goals, articulated primarily by a small group of Negroes with middle-class aspirations or status. Their kind of integration has meant that a few blacks "make it," leaving the black community, sapping it of leadership potential and know-how. As we noted in Chapter I, those token Negroes—absorbed into a white mass—are of no value to the remaining black masses. They become meaningless show-pieces for a conscience-soothed white society. Such people will state that they would prefer to be treated "only as individuals, not as

Negroes"; that they "are not and should not be preoccupied with race." This is a totally unrealistic position. In the
first place, black people have not suffered as individuals but
as members of a group; therefore, their liberation lies in
group action. This is why SNCC—and the concept of Black
Power—affirms that helping *individual* black people to solve
their problems on an *individual* basis does little to alleviate
the mass of black people. Secondly, while color blindness
may be a sound goal ultimately, we must realize that race
is an overwhelming fact of life in this historical period.
There is no black man in this country who can live "simply
as a man." His blackness is an ever-present fact of this
racist society, whether he recognizes it or not. It is unlikely
that this or the next generation will witness the time when
race will no longer be relevant in the conduct of public
affairs and in public policy decision-making. To realize
this and to attempt to deal with it does not make one a
racist or overly preoccupied with race; it puts one in the
forefront of a significant *struggle*. If there is no intense
struggle today, there will be no meaningful results tomorrow.

"Integration" as a goal today speaks to the problem of
blackness not only in an unrealistic way but also in a
despicable way. It is based on complete acceptance of the
fact that in order to have a decent house or education,
black people must move into a white neighborhood or send
their children to a white school. This reinforces, among
both black and white, the idea that "white" is automatically superior and "black" is by definition inferior. For
this reason, "integration" is a subterfuge for the maintenance of white supremacy. It allows the nation to focus
on a handful of Southern black children who get into white
schools at a great price, and to ignore the ninety-four percent who are left in unimproved all-black schools. Such situations will not change until black people become equal in

a way that means something, and integration ceases to be a one-way street. Then integration does not mean draining skills and energies from the black ghetto into white neighborhoods. To sprinkle black children among white pupils in outlying schools is at best a stop-gap measure. The goal is not to take black children out of the black community and expose them to white middle-class values; the goal is to build and strengthen the black community.

"Integration" also means that black people must give up their identity, deny their heritage. We recall the conclusion of Killian and Grigg: "At the present time, integration as a solution to the race problem demands that the Negro foreswear his identity as a Negro." The fact is that integration, as traditionally articulated, would abolish the black community. The fact is that what must be abolished is not the black community, but the dependent colonial status that has been inflicted upon it.

The racial and cultural personality of the black community must be preserved and that community must win its freedom while preserving its cultural integrity. Integrity includes a pride—in the sense of self-acceptance, not chauvinism—in being black, in the historical attainments and contributions of black people. No person can be healthy, complete and mature if he must deny a part of himself; this is what "integration" has required thus far. This is the essential difference between integration as it is currently practiced and the concept of Black Power.

The idea of cultural integrity is so obvious that it seems almost simple-minded to spell things out at this length. Yet millions of Americans resist such truths when they are applied to black people. Again, that resistance is a comment on the fundamental racism in the society. Irish Catholics took care of their own first without a lot of apology for doing so, without any dubious language from timid leadership about guarding against "backlash." Everyone understood it to be a perfectly legitimate procedure. Of course, there would be "backlash." Organization begets counterorganization, but this was no reason to defer.

The so-called white backlash against black people is something else: the embedded traditions of institutional racism being brought into the open and calling forth overt manifestations of individual racism. In the summer of 1966, when the protest marches into Cicero, Illinois, began, the black people knew they were not allowed to live in Cicero and the white people knew it. When blacks began to demand the right to live in homes in that town, the whites simply reminded them of the status quo. Some people called this "backlash." It was, in fact, racism defending itself. In the black community, this is called "White folks showing their color." It is ludicrous to blame black people for what is simply an overt manifestation of white racism. Dr. Martin Luther King stated clearly that the protest marches were not the cause of the racism but merely exposed a long-term cancerous condition in the society.

We come now to the rhetoric of coalition as part of the traditional approach to ending racism: the concept of the civil rights movement as a kind of liaison between the powerful white community and a dependent black community. "Coalition" involves the whole question of how one approaches politics and political alliances. It is so basic to an understanding of Black Power that we will devote an entire chapter to the subject.

C H A P T E R | I I I

THE MYTHS

◑ There is a strongly held view in this society that the best—indeed, perhaps the only—way for black people to win their political and economic rights is by forming coalitions with liberal, labor, church and other kinds of sympathetic organizations or forces, including the "liberal left" wing of the Democratic Party. With such allies, they could influence national legislation and national social patterns; racism could thus be ended. This school sees the "Black Power Movement" as basically separatist and unwilling to enter alliances. Bayard Rustin, a major spokesman for the coalition doctrine, has written:

Southern Negroes, despite exhortations from SNCC to

# of Coalition

organize themselves into a Black Panther Party, are going to stay in the Democratic party—to them it is the party of progress, the New Deal, the New Frontier, and the Great Society—and they are right to stay.[1]

Aside from the fact that the name of the Lowndes County Freedom Party (which will be discussed in a later chapter) is *not* the "Black Panther Party," SNCC has often stated that it does not oppose the formation of political coalitions *per se*; obviously they are necessary in a pluralistic society. But coalitions with whom? On what terms? And for what objectives? All too frequently, coalitions involving black

[1] Bayard Rustin, "Black Power and Coalition Politics," *Commentary* (September, 1966).

people have been only at the leadership level; dictated by terms set by others; and for objectives not calculated to bring major improvement in the lives of the black masses.

In this chapter, we propose to reexamine some of the assumptions of the coalition school, and to comment on some instances of supposed alliance between black people and other groups.[2] In the process of this treatment, it should become clear that the advocates of Black Power do *not* eschew coalitions; rather, we want to establish the grounds on which we feel political coalitions can be viable.

The coalitionists proceed on what we can identify as three myths or major fallacies. *First*, that in the context of present-day America, the interests of black people are identical with the interests of certain liberal, labor and other reform groups. Those groups accept the legitimacy of the basic values and institutions of the society, and fundamentally are not interested in a major reorientation of the society. Many adherents to the current coalition doctrine recognize this but nevertheless would have black people coalesce with such groups. The assumption—which is a myth—is this: what is good for America is automatically good for black people. *The second myth* is the fallacious assumption that a viable coalition can be effected between the politically and economically secure and the politically and economically insecure. *The third myth* assumes that political coalitions are or can be sustained on a moral, friendly, sentimental basis; by appeals to conscience. We will examine each of these three notions separately.

■

The major mistake made by exponents of the coalition theory is that they advocate alliances with groups which have never had as their central goal the necessarily total

---

[2] Chapter IV will be devoted to a case study of the Mississippi Freedom Democratic Party as a classic example of what can happen when black people rely on their white political "allies."

revamping of the society. At bottom, those groups accept the American system and want only—if at all—to make peripheral, marginal reforms in it. Such reforms are inadequate to rid the society of racism.

Here we come back to an important point made in the first chapter: the overriding sense of superiority that pervades white America. "Liberals," no less than others, are subjected and subject to it; the white liberal must view the racial scene through a drastically different lens from the black man's. Killian and Grigg were correct when they said in *Racial Crisis in America:*

> . . . most white Americans, even those white leaders who attempt to communicate and cooperate with their Negro counterparts, do not see racial inequality in the same way that the Negro does. The white person, no matter how liberal he may be, exists in the cocoon of a white-dominated society. Living in a white residential area, sending his children to white schools, moving in exclusively white social circles, he must exert a special effort to expose himself to the actual conditions under which large numbers of Negroes live. Even when such exposure occurs, his perception is likely to be superficial and distorted. The substandard house may be overshadowed in his eyes by the television aerial or the automobile outside the house. Even more important, he does not perceive the subjective inequalities inherent in the system of segregation because he does not experience them daily as a Negro does. Simply stated, the white American lives almost all of his life in a white world. The Negro American lives a large part of his life in a white world also, but in a world in which he is stigmatized [p. 73].

Our point is that no matter how "liberal" a white person might be, he cannot ultimately escape the overpowering influence—on himself and on black people—of his whiteness in a racist society.

Liberal whites often say that they are tired of being told "you can't understand what it is to be black." They claim to recognize and acknowledge this. Yet the same liberals will often turn around and tell black people that they should ally themselves with those who can't understand, who share a sense of superiority based on whiteness. The fact is that most of these "allies" neither look upon the blacks as co-equal partners nor do they perceive the goals as any but the adoption of certain Western norms and values. Professor Milton M. Gordon, in his book, *Assimilation in American Life*, has called those values "Anglo-conformity" (p. 88). Such a view assumes the "desirability of maintaining English institutions (as modified by the American Revolution), the English language, and English-oriented cultural patterns as dominant and standard in American life." Perhaps one holding these views is not a racist in the strict sense of our original definition, but the end result of his attitude is to sustain racism. As Gordon says:

> The non-racist Anglo-conformists presumably are either convinced of the *cultural* superiority of Anglo-Saxon institutions as developed in the United States, or believe simply that regardless of superiority or inferiority, since English culture has constituted the dominant framework for the development of American institutions, newcomers should expect to adjust accordingly [pp. 103–104].

We do not believe it possible to form meaningful coalitions unless both or all parties are not only willing but believe it absolutely necessary to challenge Anglo-conformity and other prevailing norms and institutions. Most liberal groups with which we are familiar are not so willing at this time. If that is the case, then the coalition is doomed to frustration and failure.

The Anglo-conformity position assumes that what is good for America—whites—is good for black people. We reject this. The Democratic Party makes the same claim. But the political and social rights of black people have been and always will be negotiable and expendable the moment they conflict with the interests of their "allies." A clear example of this can be found in the city of Chicago, where Mayor Daley's Democratic "coalition" machine depends on black support and unfortunately black people vote consistently for that machine. Note the results, as described by Banfield and Wilson in *City Politics:*

> The civic projects that Mayor Daley inaugurated in Chicago—street cleaning, street lighting, road building, a new airport, and a convention hall, for example—were shrewdly chosen. They were highly visible; they benefited the county as well as the city; for the most part they were noncontroversial; they did not require much increase in taxes; and they created many moderately paying jobs that politicians could dispense as patronage. The *mayor's program conspicuously neglected the goals of militant Negroes,* demands for the enforcement of the building code, and (until there was a dramatic exposé) complaints about police inefficiency and corruption. *These things were all controversial, and, perhaps most important, would have no immediate, visible result; either they would benefit those central-city voters whose loyalty could be counted upon anyway* or else (as in the case of police reform) they threatened to hurt the machine in a vital spot [p. 124; author's italics].

As long as the black people of Chicago—and the same can be said of cities throughout the country—remain politically dependent on the Democratic machine, their interests will be secondary to that machine.

Organized labor is another example of a potential ally who has never deemed it essential to question the society's basic values and institutions. The earliest advocates of unionism believed in the doctrine of *laissez faire.* The labor organizers of the American Federation of Labor (AFL) did not want the government to become involved in labor's problems, and probably for good reason. The government then—in the 1870's and 1880's—was anti-labor, pro-man-

agement. It soon became clear that political power would
be necessary to accomplish some of the goals of organized
labor, especially the goals of the railroad unions. The AFL
pursued that power and eventually won it, but generally
remained tied to the values and principles of the society as
it was. They simply wanted in; the route lay through collective bargaining and the right to strike. The unions set
their sights on immediate bread-and-butter issues, to the
exclusion of broader goals.

With the founding and development of mass industrial
unionism under the Congress of Industrial Organizations
(CIO), we began to see a slight change in overall union
orientation. The CIO was interested in a wider variety of
issues—foreign trade, interest rates, even civil rights issues
to an extent—but it too never seriously questioned the
racist basis of the society. In *Politics, Parties and Pressure
Groups*, Professor V. O. Key, Jr. has concluded: ". . . on
the fundamental question of the character of the economic
system, the dominant labor ideology did not challenge the
established order." Professor Selig Perlman wrote: ". . . it
is a labor movement upholding capitalism, not only in
practice, but in principle as well." [3] Organized labor, so
often pushed as a potential ally by the coalition theorists,
illustrates the pitfalls of the first myth; as we shall see later
in this chapter, its history also debunks the second myth.

Yet another source of potential alliance frequently cited
by the exponents of coalitions is the liberal-reform movement, especially at the local political level. But the various
reform-politics groups—particularly in New York, Chicago
and California—frequently are not tuned in to the primary
goals of black people. They establish their own goals and
then demand that black people identify with them. When
black leaders begin to articulate goals in the interest of

[3] Selig Perlman, "The Basic Philosophy of the American Labor Movement," *Annals of the American Academy of Political & Social Science*,
Vol. 274 (1951), pp. 57–63.

black people *first*, the reformers tend, more often than not, to term this "racist" and to drop off. Reformers push such "good government" programs as would result in posts being filled by professional, middle-class people. Wilson stated in *The Amateur Democrat*, "Blue-ribbon candidates would be selected, not only for the important, highly visible posts at the top of the ticket, but also for the less visible posts at the bottom" (p. 128). Black people who have participated in local reform politics—especially in Chicago—have come from the upper-middle class. Reformers generally reject the political practice of ticket balancing, which means that they tend to be "color blind" and wish to select candidates only on the basis of qualifications, of merit. In itself this would not be bad, but their conception of a "qualified" person is usually one who fits the white middle-class mold. Seldom, if ever, does one hear of the reformers advocating representation by grass-roots leaders from the ghettos: these are hardly "blue-ribbon" types. Again, when reformers push for elections at large as opposed to election by district, they do not increase black political power. "Blue-ribbon" candidates, government by technical experts, elections at large —all these common innovations of reformers do little for black people.

Francis Carney concludes from his study of California's liberal-reform Democratic clubs [4] that although those groups were usually strong on civil rights, they were nonetheless essentially middle-class oriented. This could only perpetuate a paternalistic, colonial relationship—doing *for* the blacks. Thus, even when the reformers are bent on making significant changes in the system, the question must be asked if that change is consistent with the views and interests of black people—as perceived by those people.

Frequently, we have seen that a staunch, militant stand

[4] Francis Carney, *The Rise of the Democratic Clubs in California*, Eagleton Institute Cases in Practical Politics. New York: McGraw-Hill, 1959.

taken by black leaders has frightened away the reformers.
The latter could not understand the former's militancy.
"Amateur Democrats (reformers) are passionately com-
mitted to a militant stand on civil rights, but they shy
away from militant Negro organizations because they find
them 'too race-conscious' " (p. 285), says Wilson in *The
Amateur Democrat*, citing as one example the Independent
Voters of Illinois, who felt they could not go along with
the desire of some black members to take a very strong,
pro-civil rights and anti-Daley position. The liberal-reform
politicians have not been able fully to accept the necessity
of black people speaking forcefully and for themselves.
This is one of the greatest points of tension between these
two sets of groups today; this difference must be resolved
before viable coalitions can be formed between the two.

To sum up our rejection of the first myth: As we established in Chapters I and II, the political and economic institutions of this society must be completely revised if the
political and economic status of black people is to be improved. We do not see how those same institutions can be
utilized—through the mechanism of coalescing with some
of them—to bring about that revision. We do not see how
black people can form effective coalitions with groups which
are not willing to question and condemn the racist institutions which exploit black people; which do not perceive
the need for, and will not work for, basic change. Black
people cannot afford to assume that what is good for white
America is automatically good for black people.

■

The second myth we want to deal with is the assumption
that a politically and economically secure group can collab-
orate with a politically and economically insecure group.
Our contention is that such an alliance is based on very
shaky grounds. By definition, the goals of the respective
parties are different.

Black people are often told that they should seek to form coalitions after the fashion of those formed with so-called Radical Agrarians—later Populists—in the latter part of the nineteenth century. In 1886, the Colored Farmers' Alliance and Cooperative Union was formed, interestingly enough, by a white Baptist minister in Texas. The platform of this group was similar to that of the already existing Northern and Southern Farmers' Alliances, which were white. But upon closer examination, one could see substantial differences in interests and goals. The black group favored a Congressional bill (The Lodge Federal Elections Bill) which aimed to guarantee the voting rights of Southern black people; the white group opposed it. In 1889, a group of black farmers in North Carolina accused the Southern Alliance of setting low wages and influencing the state legislature to pass discriminatory laws. Two years later, the Colored Alliance called for a strike of black cotton pickers. Professors August Meier and Elliot Rudwick ask a number of questions about these two groups, in *From Plantation to Ghetto:*

> Under what circumstances did Negroes join and to what extent, if any, was participation encouraged (or even demanded) by white employers who were members of the Southern Alliance? . . . Is it possible that the Colored Alliance was something like a company union, disintegrating only when it became evident that the Negro tenant farmers refused to follow the dictates of their white employers? . . . And how was it that the Alliance men and Populists were later so easily led into extreme anti-Negro actions? In spite of various gestures to obtain Negro support, attitudes such as those exhibited in North Carolina and on the Lodge Bill would argue that whatever interracial solidarity existed was not firmly rooted [pp. 158–59].

The fact is that the white group was relatively more secure than the black group. As C. Vann Woodward writes in *Tom Watson, Agrarian Rebel,* "It is undoubtedly true that the Populist ideology was dominantly that of the landowning farmer, who was, in many cases, the exploiter of landless tenant labor" (p. 18). It is difficult to perceive the basis on which the two could coalesce and create a meaningful alliance for the landless, insecure group. It is no surprise, then, to learn of the anti-black actions mentioned above and to realize that the relation of blacks to Populists was not the harmonious arrangement some people today would have us believe.

It is true that black people in St. Louis and Kansas backed the Populists in the election of 1892, and North Carolina blacks supported them in 1896. But it is also true that the Populists in South Carolina, under the leadership of "Pitchfork" Ben Tillman, race-baited the black man. In some places—like Georgia—the Populists "fused" with the lily-white wing of the Republican Party, not with the so-called black-and-tan wing.

Or take the case of Tom Watson. This Populist from Georgia was at one time a staunch advocate of a united front between Negro and white farmers. In 1892, he wrote: "You are kept apart that you may be separately fleeced of your earnings. You are made to hate each other because upon that hatred is rested the keystone of the arch of financial despotism which enslaves you both. You are deceived and blinded that you may not see how this race antagonism perpetuates a monetary system which beggars both." [5]

But this is the same Tom Watson who, only a few years later and because the *political* tide was flowing against such an alliance, did a complete turnabout. At that time, Democrats were disfranchising black people in state after state. But, as John Hope Franklin recorded in *From Slavery to Freedom*, "Where the Populists were unable to control

[5] Tom Watson, "The Negro Question in the South," *Arena*, Vol. 6 (1892), p. 548.

the Negro vote, as in Georgia in 1894, they believed that
the Democrats had never completely disfranchised the
Negroes because their votes were needed if the Democrats
were to stay in power. This belief led the defeated and
disappointed Tom Watson to support a constitutional
amendment excluding the Negro from the franchise—a
complete reversal of his position in denouncing South
Carolina for adopting such an amendment in 1895" (p.
218).

Watson was willing to ally with white candidates who
were anti-Democratic-machine Democrats. With the black
vote eliminated, the Populists stood to hold the balance
of power between warring factions of the Democratic
Party. Again C. Vann Woodward spells it out in his book,
Tom Watson, Agrarian Rebel:

> He [Watson] . . . pledged his support, and the support of
> the Populists, to any anti-machine, Democratic candidate
> running upon a suitable platform that included a pledge to
> "a change in our Constitution which will perpetuate white
> supremacy in Georgia."
>
> How Watson managed to reconcile his radical democratic
> doctrine with a proposal to disfranchise a million citizens of
> his native state is not quite clear.
>
> "The white people dare not revolt so long as they can be
> intimidated by the fear of the Negro vote," he explained.
> Once the "bugaboo of Negro domination" was removed,
> however, "every white man would act according to his own
> conscience and judgment in deciding how he shall vote."
> With these words, Watson abandoned his old dream of
> uniting both races against the enemy, and took his first step
> toward the opposite extreme in racial views [pp. 371–72].

At all times, the Populists and Watson emerge as politically motivated. The history of the period tells us that the
whites—whether Populists, Republicans or Democrats—always had their own interests in mind. The black man was

little more than a political football, to be tossed and kicked around at the convenience of others whose position was more secure.

We can learn the same lesson from the politics of the city of Atlanta, Georgia today. It is generally recognized that the black vote there is crucial to the election of a mayor. This was true in the case of William B. Hartsfield, and it is no less true for the present mayor, Ivan Allen, Jr. The coalition which dominates Atlanta politics has been described thus by Professor Edward Banfield in *Big City Politics*:

> The alliance between the business-led white middle class and the Negro is the main fact of local politics and government; only within the limits that it allows can anything be done, and much of what is done is for the purpose of holding it together [p. 35].

Mayor Hartsfield put together a "three-legged stool" as a base of power. The business power structure, together with the "good government"-minded middle class that takes its lead from that power structure is one leg. The Atlanta press is another. The third leg is the black community. But something is wrong with this stool. In the first place, of course, the third leg is a hollow one. The black community of Atlanta is dominated by a black power structure of such "leaders" as we described in Chapter I: concerned primarily with protecting their own vested interests and their supposed influence with the white power structure, unresponsive to and unrepresentative of the black masses. But even this privileged group is economically and politically insecure by comparison with the other two forces with whom they have coalesced. Note this description by Banfield:

> Three associations of businessmen, *the leadership of which overlaps greatly*, play important parts in civic affairs. The Chamber of Commerce launches ideas which are often

taken up as official city policy, and it is always much involved in efforts to get bond issues approved. The Central Atlanta Association is particularly concerned with the downtown business district and has taken the lead in efforts to improve expressways, mass transit, and urban renewal. Its weekly newsletter is widely read and respected. *The Uptown Association is a vehicle used by banks and other property owners to maintain a boundary line against expansion of the Negro district. To achieve this purpose it supports nonresidential urban renewal projects* [pp.31–32, author's italics].

Atlanta's substantial black bourgeoisie cannot compete with that line-up.

The political and economic interests causing the white leaders to enter the coalition are clear. So is the fact that those interests are often diametrically opposed to the interests of black people. We need only look at what the black man has received for his faithful support of politically and economically secure "alliance partners." Banfield puts it succinctly: "Hartsfield gave the Negro practically nothing in return for his vote" (p. 30). That vote, in 1957, was nine-tenths of the 20,000 votes cast by black people.

In 1963, a group of civic leaders from the black community of Southeast Atlanta documented the injustices suffered by that community's 60,000 black people. The lengthy list of grievances included faults in the sewerage system, sidewalks needed, streets which should be paved, deficient bus service and traffic control, substandard housing areas, inadequate parks and recreation facilities, continuing school segregation and inadequate black schools. Their report stated:

Atlanta city officials have striven to create an image of Atlanta as a rapidly growing, modern, progressive city where all citizens can live in decent, healthful surroundings. This image is a blatant lie so long as the city provides no health clinics for its citizens but relies entirely upon inadequate county facilities. It is a lie so long as these health clinics are segregated and the city takes no action to end this segregation. Because of segregation, only one of the four health clinics in the South side area is available to over 60,000 Negroes. This clinic . . . is small, its equipment inadequate and outdated, and its service dangerously slow due to general overcrowding.

In 1962, the city employed 5,663 workers, 1,647 of them black, but only 200 of those did other than menial work. The document lists twenty-two departments in which, of 175 equipment operators in the Construction Department, not one was black. The city did not even make a pretense of belief in "getting ahead by burning the midnight oil": there was only one public library in the community, a single room with 12,000 volumes (mostly children's books) for 60,000 people.[6]

This is what "coalition politics" won for the black citizens of one sizeable community. Nor had the situation in Atlanta's ghettos improved much by 1966. When a so-called riot broke out in the Summerhill community, local civic groups pointed out that they had deplored conditions and called the area "ripe for riot" many months earlier.

Black people must ultimately come to realize that such coalitions, such alliances have *not* been in their interest. They are "allying" with forces clearly not consistent with the long-term progress of blacks; in fact, the whites enter the alliance in many cases precisely to impede that progress.

Labor unions also illustrate very clearly the treacherous nature of coalitions between the economically secure and insecure. From the passage of the Wagner Act in 1935 (which gave unions the right to organize and bargain collectively), unions have been consolidating their position, winning economic victories for their members, and generally developing along with the growing prosperity of the country. What about black workers during this time? Their

---

[6] "The City Must Provide. South Atlanta: The Forgotten Community," Atlanta Civic Council, 1963.

status has been one of steady deterioration rather than progress. It is common knowledge that the craft unions of AFL (printers, plumbers, bricklayers, electrical workers) have deliberately excluded black workers over the years. These unions have taken care of their own—their white own. Meanwhile, the unemployment rate of black workers has increased, doubling, in some cases, that of white workers. The unions themselves were not always innocent bystanders to this development:

> . . . The war has been over twenty years now, and instead of more Negroes joining labor unions, fewer are doing so; for the Negro, increased unionization has in too many instances meant decreased job opportunity. . . .

> When the International Brotherhood of Electrical Workers became the collective bargaining agent at the Bauer Electric Company in Hartford, Connecticut in the late forties, the union demanded and got the removal of all Negro electricians from their jobs. The excuse was advanced that, since their union contract specified "whites only," they could not and would not change this to provide continued employment for the Negroes who were at the plant before the union was recognized. Similar cases can be found in the Boilermakers' Union and the International Association of Machinists at the Boeing Aircraft Company in Seattle.[7]

Precisely *because* of union recognition, black workers *lost* their jobs.

The situation became so bad that in 1959 black workers in the AFL–CIO, under the leadership of A. Philip Randolph, organized the Negro American Labor Council (NALC). Some black workers, at least, finally accepted the reality that they had to have their own black representatives if their demands were to be made—not to mention being met. The larger body did not particularly welcome the formation of this group. Randolph told the NAACP convention in June, 1960 in St. Paul, Minnesota that "a

[7] Myrna Bain, "Organized Labor and the Negro Worker," *National Review* (June 4, 1963), p. 455.

gulf of misunderstanding" seemed to be widening between
the black community and the labor community. He further
stated: "It is unfortunate that some of our liberal friends,
along with some of the leaders of labor, even yet do not
comprehend the nature, scope, depth, and challenge of this
civil rights revolution which is surging forward in the House
of Labor. They elect to view with alarm practically any
and all criticisms of the AFL–CIO because of racial discrimination." [8]

It has become clear to many black leaders that organized
labor operates from a different set of premises and with a
different list of priorities, and that the status of black
workers does not occupy a high position on that list. In
fact, they are highly expendable, as in the political arena.
Note the following observation:

> . . . the split has even deeper causes. It arises out of the
> Negro's declaration of independence from white leadership
> and white direction in the civil rights fight—the Negro view
> today is that the whites, in labor or in other fields, are unre-
> liable race campaigners when the chips are down, and that
> only the Negro can carry through to race victories.
>
> "Negro trade unionists and workers must bear their own
> cross for their own liberation. They must make their own
> crisis decisions bearing upon their life, labor, and liberty,"
> Randolph told the NAACP.[9]

The Negro American Labor Council itself, however,
suggests that such realizations may not be sufficient. It is
our position that a viable group cannot be organized *within*
a larger association. The sub-group will have to acquiesce
to the goals and demands of the parent; it can only serve
as a conscience-pricker—because it has no independent base
of power from which to operate. Coalition between the
strong and the weak ultimately leads only to perpetuation
of the hierarchical status: superordinance and subordinance.

[8] "Labor-Negro Division Widens," *Business Week* (July 9, 1960), p. 79.
[9] Bain, *op. cit.*

It is also important to note that the craft unions of the AFL were born and consolidating their positions at the same time that this country was beginning to expand imperialistically in Latin America and in the Philippines. Such expansion increased the economic security of white union workers here. Thus organized labor has participated in the exploitation of colored peoples abroad and of black workers at home. Black people today are beginning to assert themselves at a time when the old colonial markets are vanishing; former African and Asian colonies are fighting for the right to control their own natural resources, free from exploitation by Western and American capitalism. With whom will economically secure, organized labor cast its lot—with the big businesses of exploitation or with the insecure poor colored peoples? This question gives additional significance—a double layer of meaning—to the struggle of black workers here. The answer, unfortunately, seems clear enough.

We cannot see, then, how black people, who are massively insecure both politically and economically, can coalesce with those whose position is secure—particularly when the latter's security is based on the perpetuation of the existing political and economic structure.

■

The third myth proceeds from the premise that political coalitions can be sustained on a moral, friendly or sentimental basis, or on appeals to conscience. We view this as a myth because we believe that political relations are based on self-interest: benefits to be gained and losses to be avoided. For the most part, man's politics is determined by his evaluation of material good and evil. Politics results from a conflict of interests, not of consciences.

We frequently hear of the great moral value of the pressure by various church groups to bring about passage of the Civil Rights Laws of 1964 and 1965. There is no question that significant numbers of clergy and lay groups participated in the successful lobbying of those bills, but we should be careful not to overemphasize the value of this. To begin with, many of those religious groups were available only until the bills were passed; their sustained moral force is not on hand for the all-important process of ensuring federal implementation of these laws, particularly with respect to the appointment of more federal voting registrars and the setting of guidelines for school desegregation.

It should also be pointed out that many of those same people did not feel so morally obliged when the issues struck closer to home—in the North, with housing, as an example. They could be morally self-righteous about passing a law to desegregate southern lunch counters or even a law guaranteeing southern black people the right to vote. But laws against employment and housing discrimination— which would affect the North as much as the South—are something else again. After all, ministers—North and South —are often forced out of their pulpits if they speak or act too forcefully in favor of civil rights. Their parishioners do not lose sleep at night worrying about the oppressed status of black Americans; they are not morally torn inside themselves. As Silberman said, they simply do not want their peace disrupted and their businesses hurt.

We do not want to belabor the church in particular; what we have said applies to all the other "allies" of black people. Furthermore, we do not seek to condemn these groups for being what they are so much as we seek to emphasize a fact of life: they are unreliable allies when a conflict of interest arises. Morality and sentiment cannot weather such conflicts, and black people must realize this. No group should go into an alliance or a coalition relying on the "good will" of the ally. If the ally chooses to withdraw that "good will," he can do so usually without the other being able to impose sanctions upon him of any kind.

Thus we reject the last myth. In doing so, we would re-emphasize a point mentioned in Chapter I. Some believe that there is a conflict between the so-called American Creed and American practices. The Creed is supposed to contain considerations of equality and liberty, at least certainly equal opportunity, and justice. The fact is, of course, that these are simply words which *were not even originally intended* to have applicability to black people: Article I of the Constitution affirms that the black man is three-fifths of a person.[10] The fact is that people live their daily lives making practical day-to-day decisions about their jobs, homes, children. And in a profit-oriented, materialistic society, there is little time to reflect on creeds, especially if it could mean more job competition, "lower property values," and the "daughter marrying a Negro." There is no "American dilemma," no moral hang-up, and black people should not base decisions on the assumption that a dilemma exists. It may be useful to articulate such assumptions in order to embarrass, to create international pressure, to educate. But they cannot form the basis for viable coalitions.

■

What, then, are the grounds for viable coalitions?

Before one begins to talk coalition, one should establish clearly the premises on which that coalition will be based. All parties to the coalition must perceive a *mutually* beneficial goal based on the conception of *each* party of his *own* self-interest. One party must not blindly assume that what is good for one is automatically—without question—good for the other. Black people must first ask themselves what is good *for them*, and then they can determine if the

---

[10] "Representatives and direct Taxes shall be apportioned among the several States which may be included within this Union, according to their respective Numbers, which shall be determined by adding to the whole Number of free Persons, including those bound to Service for a Term of Years, and excluding Indians not taxed, three-fifths of all other Persons."

"liberal" is willing to coalesce. They must recognize that institutions and political organizations have no consciences outside their own special interests.

Secondly, there is a clear need for genuine power bases before black people can enter into coalitions. Civil rights leaders who, in the past or at present, rely essentially on "national sentiment" to obtain passage of civil rights legislation reveal the fact that they are operating from a powerless base. They must appeal to the conscience, the good graces of the society; they are, as noted earlier, cast in a beggar's role, hoping to strike a responsive chord. It is very significant that the two oldest civil rights organizations, the National Association for the Advancement of Colored People and the Urban League, have constitutions which specifically prohibit partisan political activity. (The Congress of Racial Equality once did, but it changed that clause when it changed its orientation in favor of Black Power.) This is perfectly understandable in terms of the strategy and goals of the older organizations, the concept of the civil rights movement as a kind of liaison between the powerful white community and the dependent black community. The dependent status of the black community apparently was unimportant since, if the movement proved successful, that community was going to blend into the white society anyway. No pretense was made of organizing and developing institutions of community power within the black community. No attempt was made to create any base of organized political strength; such activity was even prohibited, in the cases mentioned above. All problems would be solved by forming coalitions with labor, churches, reform clubs, and especially liberal Democrats.

Subsequent chapters will present in detail case studies showing why such an approach is fallacious. It should, however, already be clear that the building of an independent force is necessary; that Black Power is necessary. If we do not learn from history, we are doomed to repeat it, and that is precisely the lesson of the Reconstruction era. Black people were allowed to register, to vote and to participate in politics, because it was to the advantage of powerful white "allies" to permit this. But at all times such advances flowed from white decisions. That era of black participation in politics was ended by another set of white decisions. There was no powerful independent political base in the southern black community to challenge the curtailment of political rights. At this point in the struggle, black people have no assurance—save a kind of idiot optimism and faith in a society whose history is one of racism —that if it became necessary, even the painfully limited gains thrown to the civil rights movement by the Congress would not be revoked as soon as a shift in political sentiments occurs. (A vivid example of this emerged in 1967 with Congressional moves to undercut and eviscerate the school desegregation provisions of the 1964 Civil Rights Act.) We must build that assurance and build it on solid ground.

We also recognize the potential for limited, short-term coalitions on relatively minor issues. But we must note that such approaches seldom come to terms with the roots of institutional racism. In fact, one might well argue that such coalitions on subordinate issues are, in the long run, harmful. They could lead whites and blacks into thinking either that their long-term interests do *not* conflict when in fact they do, or that such lesser issues are the *only* issues which can be solved. With these limitations in mind, and a spirit of caution, black people can approach possibilities of coalition for specific goals.

Viable coalitions therefore stem from four preconditions: (a) the recognition by the parties involved of their respective self-interests; (b) the mutual belief that each party stands to benefit in terms of that self-interest from allying with the other or others; (c) the acceptance of the fact that each party has its own independent base of power and does not depend for ultimate decision-making on a force outside itself; and (d) the realization that the coalition deals with specific and identifiable—as opposed to general and vague—goals.

The heart of the matter lies in this admonition from Machiavelli, writing in *The Prince*:

> And here it should be noted that a prince ought never to make common cause with one more powerful than himself to injure another, unless necessity forces him to it. . . . for if he wins you rest in his power, and princes must avoid as much as possible being under the will and pleasure of others.*

Machiavelli recognized that "necessity" might at times force the weaker to ally with the stronger. Our view is that those who advocate Black Power should work to minimize that necessity. It is crystal clear that such alliances can seldom, if ever, be meaningful to the weaker partner. They cannot offer the optimum conditions of a political *modus operandi*. Therefore, if and when such alliances are unavoidable, we must not be sanguine about the possibility of their leading to ultimate, substantial benefit for the weaker force.

Let black people organize themselves *first*, define their interests and goals, and then see what kinds of allies are available. Let any ghetto group contemplating coalition be so tightly organized, so strong, that—in the words of Saul Alinsky—it is an "indigestible body" which cannot be absorbed or swallowed up.[11] The advocates of Black Power are not opposed to coalitions per se. But we are *not* interested in coalitions based on myths. To the extent to which black people can form *viable* coalitions will the end results of those alliances be lasting and meaningful. There will be clearer understanding of what is sought; there will be

---

* Niccolo Machiavelli, *The Prince and the Discourses*, New York: Random House (Modern Library), 1950, p. 84.

[11] Saul Alinsky speaking at the 1967 Legal Defense Fund Convocation in New York City, May 18, 1967.

greater impetus on all sides to deliver, because there will be *mutual* respect of the power of the other to reward or punish; there will be much less likelihood of leaders selling out their followers. Black Power therefore has no connotation of "go it alone." Black Power simply says: enter coalitions only *after* you are able to "stand on your own." Black Power seeks to correct the approach to dependency, to remove that dependency, and to establish a viable psychological, political and social base upon which the black community can function to meet its needs.

■

At the beginning of our discussion of Black Power, we said that black people must redefine themselves, state new values and goals. The same holds true for white people of good will; they too need to redefine themselves and their role.

Some people see the advocates of Black Power as concerned with ridding the civil rights struggle of white people. This has been untrue from the beginning. There is a definite, much-needed role whites can play. This role can best be examined on three different, yet interrelated, levels: educative, organizational, supportive. Given the pervasive nature of racism in the society and the extent to which attitudes of white superiority and black inferiority have become embedded, it is very necessary that white people begin to disabuse themselves of such notions. Black people, as we stated earlier, will lead the challenge to old values and norms, but whites who recognize the need must also work in this sphere. Whites have access to groups in the society never reached by black people. They must get within those groups and help perform this essential educative function.

One of the most disturbing things about almost all white supporters has been that they are reluctant to go into their own communities—which is where the racism exists—and work to get rid of it. We are not now speaking of whites

who have worked to get black people "accepted," on an
individual basis, by the white society. Of these there have
been many; their efforts are undoubtedly well-intended and
individually helpful. But too often those efforts are geared
to the same false premises as integration; too often the
society in which they seek acceptance of a few black people
can afford to make the gesture. We are speaking, rather, of
those whites who see the need for basic change and have
hooked up with the black liberation movement because it
seemed the most promising agent of such change. Yet they
often admonish black people to be non-violent. They should
preach non-violence in the white community. Where possible, they might also educate other white people to the
need for Black Power. The range is great, with much depending on the white person's own class background and
environment.

On a broader scale, there is the very important function
of working to reorient this society's attitudes and policies
toward African and Asian countries. Across the country,
smug white communities show a poverty of awareness, a
poverty of humanity, indeed, a poverty of ability to act in
a civilized manner toward non-Anglo human beings. The
white middle-class suburbs need "freedom schools" as
badly as the black communities. Anglo-conformity is a
dead weight on their necks too. All this is an educative role
crying to be performed by those whites so inclined.

The organizational role is next. It is hoped that eventually
there will be a coalition of poor blacks and poor whites.
This is the only coalition which seems acceptable to us,
and we see such a coalition as the major internal instru-
ment of change in the American society. It is purely academic today to talk about bringing poor blacks and poor
whites together, but the task of creating a poor-white
power block dedicated to the goals of a free, open society—
not one based on racism and subordination—must be attempted. The main responsibility for this task falls upon

whites. Black and white *can* work together in the white community where possible; it is not possible, however, to go into a poor Southern town and talk about "integration," or even desegregation. Poor white people are becoming more hostile—not less—toward black people, partly because they see the nation's attention focused on black poverty and few, if any, people coming to them.

Only whites can mobilize and organize those communities along the lines necessary and possible for effective alliances with the black communities. This job cannot be left to the existing institutions and agencies, because those structures, for the most part, are reflections of institutional racism. If the job is to be done, there must be new forms created. Thus, the political modernization process must involve the white community as well as the black.

It is our position that black organizations should be black-led and essentially black-staffed, with policy being made by black people. White people can and do play very important supportive roles in those organizations. Where they come with specific skills and techniques, they will be evaluated in those terms. All too frequently, however, many young, middle-class, white Americans, like some sort of Pepsi generation, have wanted to "come alive" through the black community and black groups. They have wanted to be where the action is—and the action has been in those places. They have sought refuge among blacks from a sterile, meaningless, irrelevant life in middle-class America. They have been unable to deal with the stifling, racist, parochial, split-level mentality of their parents, teachers, preachers and friends. Many have come seeing "no difference in color," they have come "color blind." But at this time and in this land, color *is* a factor and we should not overlook or deny this. The black organizations do not need this kind of idealism, which borders on paternalism. White people working in SNCC have understood this. There are white lawyers who defend black civil rights workers in court, and white activists who support indigenous black movements across the country. Their function is not to lead or to set policy or to attempt to define black people to black people. Their role is supportive.

Ultimately, the gains of our struggle will be meaningful only when consolidated by viable coalitions between blacks and whites who accept each other as co-equal partners and who identify their goals as politically and economically similar. At this stage, given the nature of the society, distinct roles must be played. The charge that this approach is "anti-white" remains as inaccurate as almost all the other public commentary on Black Power. There is nothing new about this; whenever black people have moved toward genuinely independent action, the society has distorted their intentions or damned their performance. The story to be told in the next chapter illustrates this point as well as all our major theses thus far.

MISSISSIPPI FREEDOM DEMOCRATS:

◐ In the first three chapters, we attempted to outline the premises for the kinds of political action which black people in this country must pursue. Clearly, that action must include the development of new political structures, new forms in order to deal with old, long-standing problems. In this chapter, we shall examine one such form: the Mississippi Freedom Democratic Party (MFDP).

As we do this, it should become clear why black people are or ought to be leery of meaningless coalitions—coalitions put together essentially for the purpose of maintaining a "united liberal image"; coalitions which do not and cannot speak to the real needs of the black people.

Bankruptcy of the Establishment

The roots of the MFDP lie in the work and philosophy of the Student Nonviolent Coordinating Committee (SNCC) which started its first voter registration project in McComb, Mississippi, in 1961. Voter registration schools were established to urge and assist people to register to vote. SNCC believed that in order to break through racist Mississippi society, black people must awaken their potential political power. Organizing around the vote was a key to this, as were demonstrations to desegregate public facilities. Unlike some other civil rights groups, SNCC saw that such demonstrations were political in character. For SNCC, desegregation became not an end in itself but part of the effort to arouse people and develop momentum to push for political power. SNCC had Black Power in mind long before the phrase was used.

SNCC did not share the naïve notion that Mississippi was an "illegitimate" state; that it was completely out of step and tune with the rest of the country. In Mississippi physical and economic reprisals, as well as political trickery, oppressed and suppressed black people. But this simply represented visible racism. The same forces operated throughout the country. It was so in 1876 when northern troops were pulled out of the South and in 1890 when a new and discriminatory Mississippi Constitution was written disfranchising blacks. It has remained so ever since. In 1890, there were 71,000 *more* registered blacks than whites; by 1964, black registration had been reduced to only 6.7 percent of the 400,000 voting-age black people.[1]

The agent of this political disfranchisement was the white racist-segregationist Mississippi Democratic Party, the major political force in the state. It supported the suppression of black people in every way. The Mississippi Democratic Party kept black people from power; it saw to it that black people never entered the political arena. In the fall of 1963, SNCC worked to build parallel political structures to challenge that stranglehold. The "Freedom Vote" held in November of that year tested the possibilities of parallelism. Over 80,000 people in the black community cast ballots for two "freedom" candidates as Governor and Lieutenant Governor.

After passage of the 1964 Civil Rights Law, SNCC decided to devote its resources to building grass-roots political strength. The decision was finally made in February, 1964 to establish a new political entity in the state of Mississippi. Formally constituted on April 26 in Jackson, it took the

[1] Report on Negro Voter-Registration in the South by the Voter Education Project of the Southern Regional Council, Atlanta, Georgia. Issued April 1, 1964.

name of the Mississippi Freedom Democratic Party
(MFDP): "Democratic" because its objective was recognition by the national party of the MFDP as the official
Democratic party in the state. Recognition would have
made the MFDP the official political party controlling the
politics and receiving the patronage of that state. The
MFDP would have been an open party, which the "regular"
party was not. This would have permitted the black people
in Mississippi to participate in politics and to begin
making decisions that affected their daily lives. This would
indeed have broadened the base of political participation,
in line with the concept of political modernization. With
these goals in mind, the MFDP spent the summer building
its numbers and strength for the national Democratic Convention which would open in August, 1964, at Atlantic City,
New Jersey.

Organizing and pursuing the goals of the MFDP was, in
essence, one of the first attempts to build a viable coalition
with the so-called liberal forces. The MFDP knew it would
have to bring external pressure to bear on the national party
if the MFDP was to have its delegates instead of the
"regulars" seated at the Convention. Various northern state
delegations stood to gain from supporting the MFDP: re-
placing the regulars could be the first step toward dislodg-
ing power from the hands of the southern senior senators
and representatives who held powerful committee positions
in the Congress. With such political benefits in mind, the
Michigan delegation passed a resolution of support on June
14, and the New York delegation on June 15. By the time
the convention opened, nine state delegations had passed
such resolutions. Endorsement was also forthcoming from
the UAW (Walter Reuther) and the ADA (Americans for
Democratic Action). Church groups and Reform Democrats also rallied.

The MFDP mounted an intensive lobbying campaign at

Atlantic City. A legal brief was prepared to be presented to the Credentials Committee of the convention; it detailed the ways in which the "regular" Mississippi Democrats had maintained their position in the state and the nation by imposing a reign of terror on black people. "Every delegate from every likely state was provided with a copy of the brief to the credentials committee. Every request for information and justification was filled. MFDP, with the help of SNCC, produced brochures, mimeographed biographies of the MFDP delegates, histories of the MFDP, legal arguments, historical arguments, moral arguments, and distributed them to the delegates.[2]

The MFDP stressed four main points at the Convention:

1. It was an open political party. It excluded no one because of race, creed or color.

2. It supported the platform of the national Democratic party. On June 30, 1964, the "regular" party had rejected the national party platform.

3. It was willing to sign the oath to remain loyal to the national party. Only four out of sixty-eight "regulars" signed such a pledge.

4. It supported and would actively campaign for the national Democratic candidates. The "regular" delegates did not; in fact, they later campaigned for the Republican candidates and helped to deliver that state to Goldwater in November, 1964.

The major counter-charge presented by the "regulars" was that the MFDP delegates were chosen illegally; that the precinct, county and state conventions they held were "outside the law." This was ludicrous at best, because the "regular" state party had been choosing delegates illegally for years, even to the extent of excluding not only blacks

---

[2] Jack Minnis, "The Mississippi Freedom Democratic Party: A New Declaration of Independence," *Freedomways*, Vol. 5, No. 2 (Spring, 1965).

but many whites. The "regular" state party made no pretense of holding open, local conventions. When Mississippi blacks attempted to attend the precinct and county meetings of the "regular" party, it was often impossible for them even to locate the meeting place. In eight precincts in six different counties, MFDP representatives went to polling stations at the time designated for the meeting but were unable to find any evidence of a meeting. Some officials denied knowledge of such a gathering; others claimed the meeting had already been held. In six different counties where meetings were held, MFDP people were refused entrance. In the town of Hattiesburg, the black people were told that they could not participate without showing poll tax receipts, despite a recent Constitutional amendment outlawing such a requirement. In ten precincts of five different counties, black Mississippians were allow to attend but their participation was restricted: some were not allowed to vote, others were not permitted to nominate delegates from the floor. The MFDP, on the other hand, held open conventions and excluded no one. They abided by the law *legally*; they did not control the law *politically*.

The national party's answer to the MFDP was, of course, "No." Intense pressure had been brought to bear on the delegates from the White House itself, and under it the "coalition" dissolved. Most of the MFDP's allies meekly dropped away and joined those who sought to bring the MFDP delegates to their knees. Several delegates told SNCC workers that they could not afford to buck the Johnson-Humphrey team.

When pushed to the wall in this manner, these delegates would frankly admit they stood to reap such a significant political and material gain from Humphrey's vice-presidency that they could not take the chance of supporting the MFDP, having it win and thus deny to Humphrey the vice-presidential nomination. . . . *these Humhprey supporters*

*were convinced that suppression of the MFDP was the price
of the vice-presidency for Humphrey.*)[3] (Authors' italics)

The rewards and punishments to be had from the Administration far outweighed anything the powerless black
people of Mississippi could do for or against them. At one
point, the MFDP reportedly had sufficient support within
the Credentials Committee to get its demands on the floor
of the Convention and to force a roll-call vote, which might
well have seated the black delegates. But once the White
House machinery went into motion, that support did a
swift fade-out.

Thus, a few members of the Credentials Committee filed
a Minority Report, but most went along with the so-called
compromise offered to the MFDP whereby the Convention
would seat two of their delegates—already picked for them
—as delegates-at-large. Great pressure was brought on the
MFDP, in turn, to accept the compromise. It did not, for
to do so would have meant revising its basic goal. The
Freedom Democrats went to Atlantic City *to replace the
racist Mississippi party, not to join it!* In effect the "compromise" called upon the MFDP to stand with the regular
party, which meant to emulate its racist politics. This was
an impossible contradiction. The MFDP could not become
part of something to which it stood in total opposition. It
was willing to accept a genuine compromise, such as that
proposed by Congresswoman Edith Green of Oregon,
whereby *loyal* Democrats of both delegations would be
seated. But the proposal which finally emerged was no
compromise. The two MFDP delegates were not to be
seated as representatives. Supposedly, the two guest seats
were "of great symbolic value." But the MFDP did not go
to the Convention as a symbolic act; it went in a sincere
effort to become part of the national Democratic party.

[3] *Ibid.*

(Even after being rejected at Atlantic City, the MFDP returned to campaign for the Johnson-Humphrey ticket: the political loyalty of the black people seemed limitless.) In return for their loyalty, the national party upheld a state party which had passed the following resolution on July 28, 1964:

> We oppose, condemn and deplore the Civil Rights Act of 1964. . . . We believe in separation of the races in all phases of our society. It is our belief that the separation of the races is necessary for the peace and tranquility of all the people of Mississippi and the continuing good relationship which has existed over the years. . . .
>
> We express our admiration and appreciation of Governor Ross B. Barnett and Governor G. Wallace of Alabama for their able, courageous, patriotic and effective work in awakening the American people to the utter necessity of the return of this country to true Constitutional Government and individual freedom. We are greatly indebted to Governor Wallace for his tremendous visit to Mississippi, and he and Gov. Barnett occupy a permanent place in the heart of every true Mississippian.

If anything was a symbolic act, it was the stand taken by the national party: a stand which clearly said "betrayal" and clearly symbolized the bankruptcy of the Establishment.

These points were never made in the press. What emerged from the media was that the MFDP constituted a kind of radical band of black people who did not understand American politics. Morally correct, perhaps, but politically unsophisticated. But the black people of the MFDP were being very sophisticated according to *their* conception of political reality; long years of put-off and denials, years of betrayal by whites and those blacks who had allied with whites. *Reality*—lessons learned through cold, hard years of suffering and political sell-out—told them that they had to stop the pattern of compromise, that they must not compromise this time just to preserve someone else's liberal image. They were not naïve or irresponsible. Accepting the humiliating "compromise" would have been the height of irresponsibility to the people they represented. Many of them realized that politics may well be the "art of compromise," but they also knew that this particular compromise held no substance; that the only hope for black people lay in a new approach. Those who doubt the wisdom of this might consider what happened to the second bone tossed to the MFDP in the convention "compromise": a directive that the national Democratic party take steps to guarantee an end to discrimination in future Mississippi Democratic conventions. Yes, an "Equal Rights Committee" was set up to do this—and in April, 1967, it met. Its conclusion: that the existence of discrimination was a matter for the Credentials Committee to determine at the next national convention!

Thus ended the first stage in the attempt to challenge an illegal state political structure outside that structure. But the challenge concept persisted; at the time, in Mississippi, it seemed the only way to demonstrate some kind of political effectiveness. This could not then be accomplished inside a state where black people could not vote. In January, 1965, the seating of five white Congressmen "elected" two months earlier was challenged; the issue came to the House floor in September. No one was particularly sanguine that this attempt would succeed. The MFDP was pleading to the same combination of national forces to rule against the Mississippi racists. Those forces had already shown their hand at the Convention.

The MFDP compiled volumes of data attesting to illegal, fraudulent "election" of the whites. But the liberals—the potential allies in the coalition—were not interested. Everyone went through the motions: laudatory speeches were made in favor of justice and against racial discrimination; the blacks were admonished that they had to "understand American politics and play by the rules of the game." The Congressional challenge was, of course, defeated—by a vote of 228 to 143. The grounds were legalistic; among them, the number of votes received by the contestants in their "unofficial, unauthorized mock election" compared to the number of votes received by the regulars in their "regular, valid, legal election." Once again, "the law" became a convenient tool to be used by illegal masters when black people sought to move. This is not a terribly surprising phenomenon in our society. Frequently, in the textbooks and classrooms, we are told that America is a "society of laws, not of men," the implication being, of course, that laws operate impartially and objectively, irrespective of race or other particular differences. This is completely inconsistent with reality. Law is the agent of those in political power; it is the product of those powerful enough to define right and wrong and to have that definition legitimized by "law." This is not to say that "might makes right," but it is to say that Might makes Law. The MFDP was operating from a base of powerlessness; thus they could be declared "illegal."

Though the MFDP was not politically naïve for the most part, a certain kind of hopeful assumption did operate—at least until Atlantic City. One might also say, as we have already suggested, that they had no other choice at that time and in that place. The chairman of the MFDP and the former director of MFDP's office in Washington have commented thus on the whole challenge concept:

In retrospect, this represented a confidence in the ultimate morality in national political institutions and practices— "They *really* couldn't know, and once we bring the facts about Mississippi to national attention, justice must surely be swift and irrevocable,"—which was a simplistic faith somewhat akin to that of the Russian peasants under the Czars. Caught in the direct kind of oppression and deprivation, the peasants would moan, "If the Czar only knew how we suffer. He is good and would give us justice. If he only knew." The fact was that he knew only too well.[4]

The lesson, in fact, was clear at Atlantic City. The major moral of that experience was not merely that the national conscience was generally unreliable but that, very specifically, black people in Mississippi and throughout this country could not rely on their so-called allies. Many labor, liberal and civil rights leaders deserted the MFDP because of closer ties to the national Democratic party. To seat the MFDP over the "regulars" would have meant a displacement of power, and it became crystal clear that in order to combat power, one needed power. Black people would have to organize and obtain their own power base before they could begin to think of coalition with others. To rely on the absolute assistance of external, liberal, labor forces was not a wise procedure.

It is absolutely imperative that black people strive to form an independent base of political power *first*. When they can control their own communities—however large or small—then other groups will make overtures to them based on a wise calculation of self-interest. The blacks will have the mobilized ability to grant or withhold from coalition. Black people must set about to build those new forms of politics.

This is the genesis of the Lowndes County Freedom Organization in Alabama, which began to be built within a year of the Atlantic City convention. Its name does not carry the word "Democratic," for the people of Lowndes did not intend to depend on the national Democratic party—or any other—for recognition. That party had clearly

[4] Lawrence Guyot and Mike Thelwell, "The Politics of Necessity and Survival in Mississippi," *Freedomways*, Vol. 6, No. 2 (Spring, 1966).

upheld racism when faced by a direct challenge. These black people knew they would have to search for and build new forms outside the Democratic party—or any other; forms that would begin to bring about the changes needed in this country.

BLACK-BELT ELECTION:

◑ There is a big sign on Highway U.S. 80 between Montgomery and Selma, Alabama, in Lowndes County. One can see it, driving west. It has the picture of a black panther on it and the words: "PULL THE LEVER FOR THE BLACK PANTHER AND GO ON HOME." This was a reminder to vote on November 8, 1966, and to vote for the candidates of the Lowndes County Freedom Organization, whose symbol is the black panther.

Some people around the country were calling this one of the most significant elections during this off-year season. In March, 1965, not one black person was even registered to vote; over the next twenty months, close to 3,900 black people had not only registered but also formed a political

New Day A'Coming

organization, held a nominating convention and slated seven of their members to run for county public office in the present election. If ever the political scientists wanted to study the phenomenon of political development or political modernization in this country, here was the place: in the heart of the "black belt," that range of Southern areas characterized by the predominance of black people and rich black soil.

Most local black people readily admit that the catalyst for change was the appearance in the county in March and April, 1965, of a handful of workers from SNCC. They had gone there almost immediately after the murder of Mrs. Viola Liuzzo, on the final night of the Selma to Mont-

gomery March. Mrs. Liuzzo, a white housewife from Detroit, had been driving marchers home when she was shot
down by Klansmen on that same Highway 80 in Lowndes
County. For the black people of Lowndes, her murder
came as no great surprise: Lowndes had one of the nation's
worst records for individual and institutional racism, a
reputation for brutality that made white as well as black
Alabama shiver. In this county, eighty-one percent black,
the whites had ruled the entire area and subjugated
black people to that rule unmercifully. Lowndes was a
prime area for SNCC to apply certain assumptions learned
over the years of work in rural, backwoods counties of the
South.

SNCC had long understood that one of the major obstacles to helping black people organize structures which
could effectively fight institutional racism was *fear*. The
history of the county shows that black people could come
together to do only three things: sing, pray, dance. Any
time they came together to do anything else, they were
threatened or intimidated. For decades, black people had
been taught to believe that voting, politics, is "white folks'
business." And the white folks had indeed monopolized
that business, by methods which ran the gamut from economic intimidation to murder.

The situation in Lowndes was particularly notable inasmuch as civil rights battles had been waged on an extensive
scale in two adjoining counties for years: in Dallas County
(Selma) and in Montgomery County. The city of Montgomery had seen a powerful movement, led by Dr. Martin
Luther King, Jr., beginning in 1955 with the bus boycott.
But Lowndes County did not appear affected by this activity. This is even more striking when one considers that at
least seventeen percent of the black people in Lowndes
work in Montgomery and at least sixty percent of the black
people do their major shopping there. Lowndes was a truly
totalitarian society—the epitome of the tight, insulated

police state. SNCC people felt that if they could help crack Lowndes, other areas—with less brutal reputations—would be easier to organize. This might be considered a kind of SNCC Domino Theory.

There were several black organizations in Lowndes County, all centered around the church: the Baptist ministerial alliances and the lodges (Eastern Star, Elks, Masons). All these groups met regularly, held functions, made decisions, collected and paid money—again laying bare the myth that black people are unorganized and unable to organize themselves. In many communities, to become head deacon of a church one must know politics, play politics, be political. The same is true of becoming and remaining Grand Master of any of the lodges. One must wheel-and-deal and constantly be involved in the internal politics of these groups. (This is, of course, no less true of most large and small groups in this society, except that many whites fail to believe black people capable of it.) Some of the most politically-oriented people who subsequently formed the Lowndes County Freedom Organization were those experienced in the internal politics of the church. The ability and power of these local leaders, however, rested inside the black community and was geared toward religious and social affairs only. Many people who were very political *inside* those organizations were unwilling to enter the *public* political arena. They were afraid.

The black people most respected by the whites in Lowndes County were the school teachers and the two high school principals. But, as in many southern communities, they were at the mercy of the white power structure. They held their positions at the sufferance of the whites; the power they had was delegated to them by the white community. And what the master giveth, the master can take away. The power of the black principals and teachers did not come from the black community, because that community was not organized around public political power. In

this sense, they were typical "Negro Establishment" figures.

The question of leadership in the county was crucial. If
there was to be a sustained political assault on racism, the
black people would have to develop a viable leadership
group. The white-established Negro leaders—the teachers,
principals—were looked up to by the black community
because they could get certain things done. They could
intercede with the white man, and they had certain overt
credentials of success: a big car, a nice house, good clothes.
The black ministers constituted another source of leadership. They have traditionally been the leaders in the black
community, but their power lay inside the black community, not with the white power structure. In some cases,
they could ask white people to do certain things for black
people, but they did not have the relative power possessed
by the white-made leaders. The ministers, likewise, could
invoke the authority of God; they were, after all, "called to
preach the gospel," and, therefore, their word had almost a
kind of divine authority in the black community.

On the other hand, the ministers knew the community
whereas the principals and some teachers did not. For the
latter, Montgomery was the drawing force, socially, while
the ministers found their social life among their congrega-
tions. Therefore they had not only a certain power, but a
great deal of influence, while the principal and teachers had
power but little influence in the community. They were
not entirely accepted; they were frequently looked upon as
"Uncle Toms," mouthing what white people said. At the
same time many ministers were caught in a vise: they did
not own their churches or the property. White people had
provided them, with heavy mortgages; if the churches were
used for purposes other than religious worship, like holding
mass meetings, the mortgages would be foreclosed, and the
ministers would be without a job.

There was another set of leaders in the black community

of Lowndes County. This was a group of middle-aged ladies, who knew the community well and were well known. They were to play a very important role in the political organization of the blacks. They had considerable influence in the black community—being staunch church members, for example—but they possessed no power at all with the white community.

Economically, Lowndes County is not noted for its equitable distribution of goods and income. The average income of blacks, most of them sharecroppers and tenant farmers, is about $985 per year. Eighty-six white families own ninety percent of the land. Inside the black community, there were in 1965 few people who had running water in their houses; only about twenty families had steam heat, and the rest got by with stove burners and wood fireplaces to keep warm. The economic insecurity of the latter is obvious, yet as we have seen, even the "Negro Establishment" faced disaster if they started meddling in "white folks' business."

Against these odds, there had somehow been in Lowndes County a long history of black men who started to fight—but were always cut down. Mr. Emory Ross, who later became an active participant in the Lowndes County Freedom Organization, had a father who was a fighter. He was shot at several times; his house riddled with bullets; his home burned down at one time. But he continued to struggle, and he was able to impart his determination to his son.

There were a few more like him. Spurred by the demonstrations and Dr. King's presence in Selma in early 1965, some seventeen brave people rallied around Mr. John Hulett, a lifelong resident of the county, to form the Lowndes County Christian Movement for Human Rights in March of that year. SNCC workers began moving around the county shortly afterward, talking a strange language: "Political power is the first step to independence

and freedom." "You can control this county politically."
It was exceptionally difficult at first to get black people to
go to the courthouse to register—the first step. The fight at
that point was waged simply in terms of being able to
establish within the black community a sense of the *right*
to fight racial oppression and exploitation. This was a battle
of no small proportion, because black people in this county
—many of them— did not even feel that they had the *right*
to fight. In addition, they felt that their fight would be
meaningless. They remembered those who had been cut
down.

From March to August, 1965, about fifty to sixty black
citizens made their way to the courthouse to register and
successfully passed the registration "test." Then, in August,
the 1965 Voting Rights Act was passed and federal "examiners" or registrars came into the county. No longer did a
black man face literacy tests or absurdly difficult questions
about the Constitution or such tactics as rejection because
one "t" was not properly crossed or an "i" inadequately
dotted. The voting rolls swelled by the hundreds. The
whites of Lowndes moved swiftly with the old weapon of
terror: some two weeks after the registrar's arrival in Hayneville, the county seat, civil rights worker Jonathan Daniels
was shotgunned to death and his fellow seminarian, Rich-
ard Morrisroe, critically wounded in Hayneville. But the
black people could not be stopped now.

The *act* of registering to vote does several things. It
marks the beginning of political modernization by broadening the base of participation. It also does something the
existentialists talk about: it gives one a sense of being. The
black man who goes to register is saying to the white man,
"No." He is saying: "You have said that I cannot vote. You
have said that this is my place. This is where I should remain. You have contained me and I am saying 'No' to your
containment. I am stepping out of bounds. I am saying 'No'
to you and thereby I am creating a better life for myself. I

am resisting someone who has contained me." That is what the first act does. The black person begins to live. He begins to create his *own* existence when he says "No" to someone who contains him.

But obviously this is not enough. Once the black man has knocked back centuries of fear, once he is willing to resist, he then must decide how best to use that vote. To listen to those whites who conspired for so many years to deny him the ballot would be a return to that previous subordinated condition. He must move independently. The development of this awareness is a job as tedious and laborious as inspiring people to register in the first place. In fact, many people who would aspire to the role of an organizer drop off simply because they do not have the energy, the stamina, to knock on doors day after day. That is why one finds many such people sitting in coffee shops talking and theorizing instead of organizing.

The question of how to utilize the vote became most pertinent in Lowndes County. Since the 1930's, history books and traditional political science treatises had concluded that the salvation of the black man lay in the Democratic party. The black people of Lowndes County had certain doubts about that, doubts based on more than conjecture. The lessons of the Mississippi Freedom Democratic Party's experience were all too clear. In Lowndes itself, black people saw the local Democratic party as the sheriff who brutalized them; as the judge in kangaroo courts who made them pay high fines. They knew that the chairman of the Lowndes County Democratic Committee, Robert Dickson, was a defendant in a federal court suit charging that he had evicted black tenant farmers from his land because they registered to vote. They saw George Wallace at the head of the state party; they saw Eugene "Bull" Connor and Sheriff Jim Clark. They knew it was absurd to demean themselves by attempting to sit down with the local Democratic politicians. If the Democratic

(or any other) party was to recognize and respect the mobilized power of black people, those people would have to
organize independently. They also recognized the psychological need of knowing that they could come together on
their own, make decisions and carry them out. Therefore,
they began to look around to see what it would mean to
run independent candidates in the elections for county offices (sheriff, tax assessor, tax collector, coroner and three
positions on the county Board of Education) to be held in
November, 1966.

The SNCC research staff discovered an unusual Alabama
law which permits a group to organize a potential political
party on a county-wide basis. To be recognized as a county
party, the group has to receive twenty percent of the votes
cast in the election for county offices. The black people of
Lowndes County and SNCC then began the hard work of
building a legitimate, independent political party with no
help from anyone else. Virtually the entire country condemned this decision; it was "separatism"; it was traditionally doomed "third-party politics" and the only way to
succeed was through one of the two established parties.
Some even said that the black voters of Lowndes County
should support the Democratic party out of gratitude for
being given the vote. But the Democratic party did not give
black people the right to vote; it simply stopped denying
black people the right to vote.

In March, 1966, the Lowndes County Freedom Organization was born with the immediate goals of running candidates and becoming a recognized party. In building the
LCFO, it was obviously wise to attempt first to recruit
those black people who owned land and were therefore
somewhat more secure economically than those without
property. But there were few of them. Those without property, merely sharecropping on white-owned plantations,
were subject to being kicked off the land for their political
activity. This is exactly what had happened at the end of

December, 1965; some twenty families were evicted and spent the rest of the winter living in tents, with temperatures often below freezing. Their fate, and it was shared by others later, intensified the fear, but it also served to instill a sense of the tremendous need to establish an independent base of group power within the community. That base could lend support, security. Thus, despite the ever-present threat of loss of home and job and even possibly life, the black people of Lowndes County continued to build. Mass meetings were held weekly, each time in a different part of the county. Unity and strength, already developing over the winter, grew.

In May, 1966, the time arrived to put up black candidates in the primary election. Around the state and the nation, many people raised the perennial question of qualifications. What black people in Lowndes County were qualified to hold public office? It was the old game of putting black people on the defensive, making the black man question his ability, his talents, himself. No one *seriously* questioned Wallace's (George or Lurleen) qualifications to be governor, or Jim Clark's to be sheriff of Dallas County, or "Bull" Connor's to be Chief of Public Safety(!) in Birmingham, Alabama. For that matter, in the 1770's the American colonists did not spend sleepless nights worrying whether they could rule themselves. This point bears emphasis, for white Western "civilization" is always projecting itself as ready whereas the black man must prepare himself. If preparation means learning to rule in the racist manner that whites demonstrated in Lowndes County and throughout this country, then black people should not bother to learn those lessons.

The black people of Lowndes County were ready and made themselves even readier. Workshops were held, with SNCC's assistance, on the duties of the sheriff, the coroner, the tax assessor, tax collector and members of the Board of Education—the offices up for election. Booklets, frequently in the form of picture books, were prepared by SNCC and distributed over the county. People began to see and understand that no college education or special training was needed to perform these functions. They called primarily for determination and common sense, and black people in Lowndes had long since shown that they possessed these qualities.

The Lowndes County Freedom Organization called a county-wide meeting to draw up its platform. This would not be the usual process whereby the platform serves as a "front," a showpiece to which party candidates give lip-service and then proceed to ignore as they wish. Here in Lowndes, the black people met, drew up their platform and then chose their candidates on the basis of which could best follow that platform.

To comply with Alabama law, the primary was scheduled for the same day as the primaries of the other parties in the state—May 3, 1966. The law also indicated that a man could vote in only one primary—a requirement which led to further attacks on the LCFO and SNCC. If black people were to support the LCFO, they must boycott the Democratic primary entirely. SNCC workers urged them to do so, in order to protect the legality of the independent primary and because of the established racism of the Alabama Democratic Party. But a new cry went up: "Alabama Negroes Told Not to Vote."

They did vote, of course—in their own primary. More than nine hundred black people came to Hayneville, the county seat, and cast their ballots. Many traveled over twenty-five miles to that seat of terror, where Jonathan Daniels had been shotgunned to death nine months earlier. They came to vote in *their* primary, to nominate *their* candidates for public office.

The nominating convention was held at the First Baptist Church, but only after a struggle. An Alabama statute (Title 17, Section 414) stipulated that primaries must be held in the vicinity of the courthouse. With this in mind, the LCFO decided to hold its nominating convention in the vacant space adjacent to the county courthouse. The sheriff prohibited this on the basis that such a meeting would "cause too much confusion." The LCFO, determined not to have their convention nullified because of failure to abide by the law, informed the United States Department of Justice of its intent to hold the convention next to the courthouse. One Justice Department representative said that if the meeting were held there, it would be a "turkey shoot."

The LCFO appealed to the Justice Department for protection, stating that if such protection were not forthcoming, the LCFO would be obliged to protect themselves. It was only after the local probate judge and the State Attorney General assured the LCFO that a convention held one half-mile from the courthouse, in the First Baptist Church, would be legal that the black people decided to hold the convention there. Thus, white officials quickly and justly interpreted the law when the rights of the Lowndes County black people were backed up with the power of organized and determined numbers.

The campaign which followed was hardly a typical American political campaign. There were no debates (or offers to debate) between the candidates; black candidates certainly did not canvass white voters and no white candidates made open appeals for black votes.

On the weekend before the election, the Lowndes County Freedom Organization prepared to meet its first electoral test. On Sunday afternoon, November 6, a meeting of seventy-five persons was held in the organization's headquarters. These were poll-watchers, election clerks, SNCC staff and local people. The duties of poll-watching were explained, and the procedure for challenging voters was discussed. Three things were stressed at the meetings: (1) The whites might attempt to challenge blacks on a mass scale; (2) The whites might attempt to vote in the name of persons who were no longer in the county or who had died—the graveyard vote; (3) Abuse of the Alabama law which provides for "helpers" had to be guarded against carefully.

What should be done if black voters were challenged? The Alabama law was clear. The challenged voter simply signs an oath stating he is a bona fide resident registered to vote, and he has another voter who owns property in the precinct witness this. Then the challenged voter votes, not on the machine but on a paper ballot. Time was spent going over names of black people in each precinct who owned property and who were neither poll-watchers nor election clerks; these persons could serve as witnesses for challenged black voters.

If the whites started challenging blacks on a mass scale, it was decided that blacks would do the same thing to whites. One person stated: "In fact, I think we ought to just challenge for the heck of it every two hours or so, just to let those crackers know that we are on our toes and they'd better not try anything." This was met with wide approval, and everyone agreed that Tuesday would be a historic day in Lowndes County: "Lord, Lord, Lord, can you imagine, black folk saying to Mr. Charlie: 'I challenge your right to vote'!"

People felt that there were many whites listed as registered who had long since moved out of the county or died. The voting list had never been purged. But even at that late date, the organization still did not have an official list of registered voters. Thus, on Sunday, two days before the election, there was no precise knowledge of exactly who was registered in the county. The most recent available list dated only to April, 1966, and some six hundred black people had registered since then. People decided to go to the probate judge's office the following morning to secure an up-to-date list.

Then the meeting turned its attention to the "helper" system. Under Alabama law, a voter may ask for assistance inside the voting booth if: (1) he is blind, (2) he is physically disabled, or (3) he "cannot read the ballot." Any person is entitled to help one voter; an election official (inspector or clerk, not a poll-watcher) may help any number of voters if asked by the voters. This was the catch. The leaders of the Lowndes County Freedom Organization knew that once a local white person got behind the curtain with a black person, that vote would be lost.

"O.K.," one person said. "The big point for us to make is that no black people should ask any white man for help. We'll help each other." There were immediate cries of agreement and "you said it, brother." "We are our brother's helper." Amen!

Then, Mr. Emory Ross, the candidate for coroner, stood up. "Instead of pulling the black panther lever and going on home, we tell our people to pull the lever and back up fifty feet and stand ready to help our brother if he needs it." The dilapidated, one-room headquarters rocked with applause. This was the high point of the five-and-a-half-hour session. These black people were, indeed, coming alive. They were being *involved* in politics—and they were learning.

There would be sixteen voting machines in the eight precincts, some precincts having as many as three, others with only one. The poll-watchers were instructed to make a log of events throughout the day: the name and race of each voter, who asked for help, who helped whom, any and all experiences at the polling place. "Let's keep writing. There's nothing like a pencil and paper to keep the other man honest. His honesty goes up at least fifty percent." Poll-watchers would work in two-hour shifts, alternating with poll-watchers on the otuside.

"For us on the outside," one person asked. "How far away do we have to be?"

Mr. Hulett, who had done his homework, quietly answered: "Thirty feet."

"Alright, that's what I want to know."

On Monday morning, Mr. Hulett went with Mr. Sidney Logan, the LCFO candidate for sheriff, to see Probate Judge Harrell Hammond at the courthouse in Hayneville. Alabama law (Title 17, Section 54) requires the Judge to prepare and send a final list of registered voters to the Alabama Secretary of State. "I don't know much about these lists and things," Mr. Hammond calmly stated. "We haven't sent any lists anywhere." The law requires that this be done shortly after the last day of registration; when was that? "Gentlemen, I really don't know. All I know is that I tried every way I know to put some colored on the voting boxes. And I did. And I got some criticism for that." Although required by Alabama law to keep a list of registered voters with notation of sex and race, this had not been done. Could the LCFO people have an official list of all registered voters? "Yes, I'll get you one now," Hammond agreed. "You can Xerox a couple of copies here. No charge for this."

The official list was handed over. It showed a total registration, broken down by precinct and voting boxes, of 5,806.

That same day, a meeting was held at 10 A.M. of all election officials and poll-watchers. Blacks and whites crowded together in the first-floor corridor of the courthouse. An official from the Election Commissioner's office in Montgomery explained the operation of the voting machine (there was a machine present) and the duties of the officials at each polling place as well as of the poll-watchers. The black people asked many questions.

A list on the bulletin board in the corridor indicated that eighty-one persons had already cast absentee ballots (seven more names were to be added on election day). The LCFO people copied the names and asked Judge Hammond the legal procedure for challenging absentee ballots. He did not know. A call was placed to the Alabama Attorney General's Office in Montgomery. The Attorney General's Office advised that the state statutes did not deal with this; there was no established procedure.

Later Monday afternoon, two officials from the United States Department of Justice stopped by at the LCFO headquarters to say there would definitely be at least two federal observers at each voting machine in the county. Their function would be merely to observe and record events. A Justice Department trailer had been set up in Hayneville next to the small post office, across the town square from the courthouse.

There was a guarded sigh of relief from the LCFO people, who then said that black people expected any and every kind of trouble from the local whites the following day. The Justice Department did not share this pessimism. They had talked to Judge Hammond "and others," and it was the general consensus of the whites in the county that the LCFO would not win the positions contested by the white Democratic party.

Now, the white Democratic party had a slate of candidates for every county office except two positions on the Board of Education. The Lowndes County Republican Party had slated candidates *only* for those two offices. This meant that the LCFO candidates for those two positions could lose only if the whites, who were predominantly Democrats, voted a split ticket: first for the Democrats and then for the two Republicans. The general opinion of the LCFO was that not enough whites would split their votes. The Justice Department offered the view that the local whites were prepared to live with the election of two black people to the Board of Education, in the belief that black people would be too "scared" to vote for Mr. Sidney Logan for sheriff.

Was this white folks' concession to the growing black

political power? Why didn't the white Democratic party slate candidates for the two Board of Education positions? (They did run a candidate for the third Board position.) Had a deal been made between the local Democrats and local Republicans? Apparently so. But if so, why did they think that white voters would be sophisticated enough to split their vote? The LCFO black leaders were cautiously optimistic. At no time did Mr. Hulett or the black candidates make public or private boasts about their ability to win. In fact, they affirmed that victory was by no means certain. They were not overly optimistic about the figures showing thousands of newly registered black people.

A mass meeting was held on Monday night at a local Baptist church, with more than 650 black people present. It was a magnificent mixture of a work-session (the audience was seated by precincts and spent more than an hour going over the voter list to note whether the listed person was white or black) and an inspirational rally. Rarely if ever before in the long struggle of black people in the South have so many spent an evening learning the sheer mechanics of voting, discussing details of getting friends and neighbors to the polls and being inspired by the short speeches of the candidates ("If you want to hear your voice, make Hinson your choice—for the Board of Education").

Mr. Hulett closed the meeting by admonishing the poll-watchers "to be at the polls tomorrow morning at seven. They open at eight; we'll be there at seven. And one other thing. I want our people to be the best-dressed there tomorrow. Let's dress up and look like people when we go to the polls tomorrow."

Only a John Hulett could have said that and not been misunderstood. Everyone understood.

There was no long discussion of Black Power at the mass meeting. Mr. Hulett talked of winning office and governing the county not in a spirit of vindictiveness but in a manner that would serve "as a model for democracy." All the un-informed editorial writers throughout the country, all the panic-stricken whites in insulated suburbs across this land should have been there that night. Here was a group of inspired black people who could not care less about the endless, senseless debates raging all summer over Black Power. This was a group of black people who were out to right centuries of wrong in their own little corner of the world. They had no naïve notions that the next twenty-four hours would usher in the millennium. "We may not win tomorrow," Mr. Hulett said, "but we won't quit. We won't give up. Some of our candidates might win and some might not, but we aren't going to get discouraged and start fussing among ourselves."

These people did not have to argue Black Power; they understood Black Power.

And after they had sung "We Shall Overcome," they got ready to go out into the dark and dangerous (reports were rife that the Klan was out on the highways) and lonely Alabama night. Home to two- and three-room shacks crowded with cots and sleeping children. Home to outside toilets and flies and mice. Tired, excited, expectant. Some talked something about an historic event for Lowndes, others just nodded and agreed and kept their shotguns close by their sides because they knew that only so much had changed. They knew that mass meetings can do only so much. They knew there was another reality, the reality that some would be kicked off the land in a few short hours; the reality of a white world outside their little mass meeting, a world that would not give up power easily. So they climbed into their cars and went on home to sleep a while. Tomorrow they had to get up early and, for the first time in Lowndes County, they had to T.C.B. (Take Care of Business—black folks' business).

Tuesday came—a good day, weatherwise, for the election. Not too hot, not raining.

Twenty-five black people were waiting at the polling place in Precinct 1 at 7:25 A.M. This was the LCFO's strongest precinct. Drivers started moving over the county, transporting people back and forth to the polls. ("Just carry a piece of white paper and hold it up on the highway. That way we'll know and we'll stop and pick you up.")

In mid-morning, reports started coming in of election violations and irregularities. Messages were left at headquarters for Mr. Hulett and the SNCC staff. "Get over to Precinct 7, trouble there. Not letting our poll-watchers observe everything. Whites going in booths with Negroes." "Check Precinct 2. Black people from plantations being given marked ballots before they go in. Against the law." "Get up to Hayneville right away. Intimidating our people outside." "Precinct 5 needs more 'helpers' badly. See what can be done."

The political truths and realities were coming home. This was not a protest demonstration. This was not a sit-in or picket line. This was electoral politics in black-belt Alabama. And the black people were in it now—to stay.

In one precinct, three black women were poll-watching. The polling place was in a back room of a store, Portis' Store. White men filled the room with cigar smoke and laughter. The election inspector ordered an LCFO lawyer out of the store. The atmosphere became tense, menacing. The three black ladies stood with their pads and clipboards, scared but *there*. They did not challenge any white voters in that hostile atmosphere. But by their mere presence they were challenging the very foundations of white power.

In another precinct, election officials would not permit federal observers to observe the "helping" process in cases where whites "helped" black voters. This denial was against the law, but the federal observers did not complain. They simply stated that it would be part of their report.

White plantation owners were bringing in "their niggers" by the truckload.

To offset these developments, a quick LCFO and SNCC strategy was developed around mid-afternoon. Since not enough black helpers could be found to go around, black people approaching the polls were advised that if they needed help from an election official, simply tell him: "I want to vote *only* the Panther ticket," or "I want to vote *only* for the Freedom Organization." That was all. Don't bother with the constitutional amendments, the other offices on the ballot. Just pull the Panther lever and go on home. This last-minute, improvised bit of voter education might have worked in a few instances, but it was probably too little and too late.

As the election day wore toward an end, the great, spirited plans of the previous Sunday seemed to dissipate in the cold, hostile, atmosphere of the white-dominated polling places. Some blacks coming to vote in Fort Deposit, in the southern section of the county, told the SNCC and LCFO people outside that they did not want any black people helping them; they were going to vote for the whites. Other blacks were aware that some of the election officials were plantation owners or owners of major credit-giving stores, and if the voters asked for help from LCFO there would be repercussions. There were a few complaints that some poll-watchers were not challenging the white voters. There was no great sense of victory in the LCFO. They did not expect the results to be favorable.

The polls closed at 6 P.M. and the LCFO headquarters slowly began to fill up with workers and candidates to await the returns. Someone brought in a television set and people watched the returns coming in around the country: New York, Michigan, Massachusetts, Illinois.

Poll-watchers from the various precincts began to bring in precinct vote counts and the totals were posted on a blackboard that ran almost the length of the room:

Office	LCFO Candidate	White Candidate
Sheriff	Sidney Logan (1,645)	Frank Ryals, Dem. (2,320)
Coroner	Emory Ross (1,612)	Jack Golson, Dem. (2,265)
Tax Assessor	Alice Moore (1,606)	Charlie Sullivan, Dem. (2,265)
Tax Collector	Frank Miles (1,605)	Iva Sullivan, Dem. (2,270)
Board of Education	Robert Logan (1,669)	David Lyons, Rep. (1,937)
Board of Education	John Hinson (1,668)	Tommie Coleman, Rep. (1,966)
Board of Education	Willie Strickland (1,602)	C. B. Haigler, Dem. (2,170)

That night, also, Mr. Andrew Jones of Fort Deposit, an active worker in the LCFO who had spent the day driving voters to the polls, was severely beaten by a group of whites while on his way home. His sixteen-year-old daughter was an eye-witness to the attack, and later gave a report at the LCFO headquarters. A couple, the Jordans (he was an election day driver, she a poll-watcher), were kicked out of the house that had been their home for eleven years— along with their nine children—by the plantation owner.

■

It was clear: the whites had split their votes after all, and a large number of blacks had voted for whites. This is what Mr. Hulett and the others knew: that the figure for registered black voters did not represent the number who would vote with the LCFO.

What had happened was simple and predictable. During the first few months after August, 1965, when the federal registrars came into the county, the "independent blacks" had flocked down by the hundreds, anxious to register and to vote for a change. But then the plantation owners began to herd in "their niggers" and to register them. When election day came, the whites could be fairly confident that they had a certain portion of the black vote tied up. This undoubtedly is the case across the Southland.

But there will always be those black people who will vote for whites against blacks because they fear economic and physical reprisal, because of an embedded belief that politics and voting are indeed "white folks' business." These people are lost. Not much time and resources should be spent trying to woo them or isolate them. The important task is to build on that core of votes already in the LCFO column. This must be done primarily from the remaining fifty-one percent yet to be registered. On Saturday and Sunday prior to election, many black people said that they had intended to register, but simply had not got around to it. The last days of registration for this election had fallen during the peak of harvesting time, and many people were in the fields trying to beat the bad weather.

The LCFO must set up precinct subdivisions and these must see to it that people are taken—literally—to the registration office. This must be followed up with periodic sessions of voter education in the sheer mechanics of the electoral process. The precinct captain must become as familiar to the residents of his precinct as the local ministers are. For so long, black communities in the Mississippi Delta and the black-belt areas have had to rely on inspirational and emotional appeals and on the tactics of protest politics. These were, in large part, successful; but now they must put together a sustained organization. The LCFO is now a recognized political party in the county; it must organize and operate as one.

The new Lowndes County Freedom Party is also aware that somehow it must counteract the economic dependence which so seriously impedes organizing. It must begin thinking of ways to build a "patronage" system—some sort of mechanism for offering day-to-day, bread-and-butter help to black people immediately in need. A prime example occurred on election day at 1 P.M., when a black family's home was completely destroyed by fire; fourteen children, ranging in age from four to eighteen, and two adults were left homeless and penniless. Immediate assistance in the form of clothes, food, and dollars coming from the Party would have been politically invaluable. It is true that the Party does not have the local resources to help every family burned out of their homes or kicked off the land or in need of a job, but it must begin to move in that direction. Such "patronage" should always be identified as coming from the Party. If necessary (and it undoubtedly will be necessary), drives in selected northern communities could be launched to help until the Party can show more substantial victories. Only so many black people will rush to the banner of "freedom" and "blackness" without seeing some way to make ends meet, to care for the children.

One way or another, the fact is that the John Huletts of the South will participate in political decision-making in their time and in their land. November 8, 1966, made one thing clear: some day black people will control the government of Lowndes County. For Lowndes is not merely a section of land and a group of people, but an idea whose time has come.

CHAPTER | VI

TUSKEGEE, ALABAMA:

◗ The town of Tuskegee, in Macon County, Alabama, is undoubtedly one of the most significant areas in the history of the black man in this country. People throughout the world know Tuskegee as the home base of Booker T. Washington, from 1881 to his death in 1915. He founded Tuskegee Institute in 1881 and he was widely acclaimed as *the* leader of black people during that period. Dr. George Washington Carver, the scientist, became a second great name; his accomplishments in the Tuskegee Institute science laboratory with peanuts and sweet potatoes made him internationally known and respected at a time when most whites and many blacks knew nothing of Dr. W. E. B. DuBois, William Monroe Trotter and other black intel-

The Politics of Deference

lectuals of that day. In 1924, the nation's first, all-black-staffed Veterans' Administration Hospital was established at Tuskegee, bringing to the county a wealth of educational and medical talent. During World War II, Tuskegee was the site of the first training base for black Air Force pilots. Then, in 1958, it became the first community to be investigated by the United States Commission on Civil Rights, set up under the 1957 Civil Rights Act.

Since the nineteenth century black people have constituted the main population of Macon County—then, and now, roughly eighty-four percent. In the post-Civil War period, blacks voted and made their vote felt at times, as we will illustrate. But in 1901, the white racist state legislature amended the state constitution and effectively disfranchised most of the black citizens. Booker T. Washington protested mildly, but subsequently acquiesced.

This chapter will describe the long, hard, successful fight waged by some in the county to regain the ballot—to regain the previous status of broadened participation in politics—and the manner in which this regained participation has been exercised. It has been exercised with "restraint," that is, the black leaders have not utilized their new position to exercise effective political power. The black leaders have pursued what we call a "politics of deference." [1] Many people there, and throughout the country, have looked on Tuskegee as a "model" of "bi-racial" government—blacks and whites working and governing together. We reject that conclusion. We see the present-day Tuskegee situation as perpetuating a racially deferential society, and we suggest that a politics of Black Power, as defined in this book, would be far healthier for the community. We suggest that Tuskegee could become a better model—North and South —for those numerous electoral districts where black people have a commanding majority.

First, let us discuss the political history of this community.

■

An entire philosophy of race relations developed around Booker T. Washington's leadership in the late nineteenth century. This philosophy encouraged black people to concentrate their time and energy on developing their educational and economic potential. It de-emphasized political activity; Washington was not noted for advocating that blacks run for public office. The good white folks would take care of the political business and as black people

---

[1] This phrase is attributed to Dr. Paul L. Puryear, former political science professor at Tuskegee, now at Fisk University.

proved themselves "worthy," they would slowly be "accepted" by their white neighbors. Always embedded in Washington's philosophy was the notion that black people had to prove themselves to white people. Lerone Bennet, Jr., has described Washington's leadership as follows in *Before the Mayflower*:

> Almost everything Washington said or did was shot through with a certain irony. He bowed before the prejudices of the meanest Southerner, but he moved in circles in the North which were closed to all but a few white men. He told Negroes that Jim Crow was irrelevant, but he himself violated the law by riding first class in Pullman cars with Southern white men and women. And irony of ironies: he who advised Negroes to forget about politics wielded more political power than any other Negro in American history [p. 277].

A most ironic aspect of Booker T. Washington's career is the context in which that career started. Tuskegee Institute itself was established precisely because, in 1880, the black people of Macon County possessed political power. As we have already stated, blacks then constituted the great majority of the county population. A former Confederate Colonel, W. F. Foster, was running for the Alabama legislature on the Democratic ticket. Obviously needing black votes, he went to the local black leader, a Republican named Lewis Adams, and made a deal: if Adams would persuade the blacks to vote for him, he would—once elected—push for a state appropriation to establish a school for black people in the county. Adams delivered; Foster was elected and a sum of $2,000 per year was appropriated to pay teachers' salaries for a school. Adams wrote to Hampton Institute in Virginia for a person to come and set up the school. The head of Hampton recommended one of his best teachers, Booker T. Washington.

Thus the black people of Tuskegee used the ballot effec-

tively to gain their goals. They were not begging, relying on
sentiment or morality; they traded their votes for a specific
and meaningful reward. If Foster had not kept his part of
the bargain, they could have "punished" him with their
political power at the next election. This kind of strength
could come only from organization and recognition of
their interests. Foster respected their Black Power. This
historical fact seems to have been forgotten by many people
today who counsel black people to follow the teachings of
Washington in regard to mitigating political activity. If
Mr. Adams and the black people had not acted politically,
Washington might never have acquired the influence he
did.

Another frequently overlooked lesson of Washington's
career concerns that aspect of his position which called
upon whites to "reward" blacks with "ultimate" inclusion
in the political process. Washington believed strongly that
once black people acquired skills useful to the southern
environment (blacksmithing, carpentry, cooking, farming,
etc.), once they acquired a sound economic base, once
they bought homes and became law-abiding citizens of the
community, the whites should and would "accept" them
as "first-class citizens." This meant, to Washington, ultimately including them as voters and public office-holders.
With this goal in mind, Washington addressed letters to
the state constitutional conventions of Louisiana (1898)
and Alabama (1901), urging them not to revise their constitutions to deny the vote to black people. He felt that any
revisions should apply equally to whites as well as blacks,
that it might be wise to exclude *all* illiterate, uneducated
people.

Southern whites did not heed his counsel. The fact is
that Washington overestimated the "good will" and "good
faith" of white America. The blacks of Tuskegee, for
the most part, did follow the teachings of the Institute's

founder. They did not concentrate on politics; they did concentrate on acquiring skills, on building an economically secure life. But they were not "rewarded" with political participation. The Institute and later the Veterans' Administration Hospital—both of which were black-staffed —had attracted to the community a black population with higher educational and economic status than in any other county of the state. These black people built fine homes and went about their business at the college or the hospital without challenging the political control of the sixteen percent white population.

A modus operandi had been reached between the Tuskegee blacks and whites: the blacks would run Tuskegee Institute and the V.A. Hospital while the whites would provide commercial services (banks and stores) and hold all political offices—thus overseeing law-enforcement, the assessing and collecting of taxes, the public school system and so forth. The accommodation was perfect, and many people throughout the country pointed to Tuskegee as a showplace of harmonious race relations. So the sizeable black middle-class society had its debutante balls and social clubs, made no great demand to take part in political decision-making, and seemed to have forgotten—or perhaps they never knew—the earlier political history of the county when black people voted and gained political benefits.

In Chapter IV, we noted that in 1890 Mississippi had been the first state of the old Confederacy to rewrite its laws so as to exclude blacks from voting—a procedure eventually adopted by virtually all of those states. In 1901, it was Alabama's turn. The state revised its constitution, purging all voters—black and white—from its rolls. It then adopted new rules for registration; these provided for a "literacy" test in which an applicant had to read, write *and interpret* a section of the U.S. or the state constitution.

Local boards of registration were set up in each county and controlled, of course, by whites; they could reject an applicant if he did not "interpret" the constitution to their satisfaction. A "voucher" system was also set up whereby two registered voters had to "vouch for" or identify the applicant. The registrars required black applicants to get white vouchers. Thus, a network of devices—ostensibly not racial, because the Fifteenth Amendment to the U.S. Constitution prohibited voting discrimination based on race— were established; this meant that black people would have a most difficult time getting back on the registration books. Needless to say, whites registered without delay or dilatory tactics on the part of the registrars. And, again needless to say, the whites soon had a majority of registered voters; White Power was firmly entrenched.

But there was always a handful of black people in the community who did not accept the politically subordinate position assigned to them. They knew they were colonial subjects in their own land. Early in the 1930's, a black sociologist joined the faculty of Tuskegee Institute; he later stated: "Booker T. Washington came to teach the Negroes how to make a living. I came to teach them how to live." [2] By this he meant that black people should become more active in civic affairs. A small group began to organize in the late 1930's to get more blacks registered. The leadership came from some thirty black men who formed the Tuskegee Men's Club. This group reorganized as the Tuskegee Civic Association (TCA) in 1941. The TCA confronted a comfortable black middle class that was satisfied to let the status quo remain and the town whites who were all too pleased with the good manners of these blacks who "knew their place." Professor Charles G. Go-

[2] Charles V. Hamilton, *Minority Politics in Black Belt Alabama*, Eagleton Institute, Cases in Practical Politics. New York: McGraw-Hill, 1962, p. 1.

million, one of the leaders of the TCA, has quoted a statement by a white public official in 1940 which sums up the nature of race relations in the county: "Sometimes some of the rural Negroes and some of the colored professors at the Institute think that we don't treat them fairly, but in general we manage to keep them pacified." [3]

Slowly, however, black names increased on the voting rolls: in 1940, there were approximately 29 registered black voters, 115 in 1946, 514 in 1950, and 855 in 1954. The figure rose against the most incredible obstacles: registrars would resign and not be replaced; black Ph.D.'s were rejected for not being able to state the precise length of time —down to the days—they had been residents. On one occasion, the Board of Registrars met in the vault of the local bank, in an attempt to avoid having to take registration applications from black applicants. This occured on April 19, 1948, and a very light-skinned person (who could "pass" for white) had to locate the meeting place of the board after several black people were refused the information.

Many educated black people chose not to become involved in this sham process. Rather than submit to constant indignities, they simply withdrew. "We just don't bother with those white folks downtown," became a common response. This was, of course, precisely what the white power structure wanted: such an attitude would never challenge their control.

Unlike other areas in the black belt, Macon County remained relatively free of overt acts of violence and intimidation during the forties and fifties. This, again, contributed to the façade of "good race relations" in the county. Only infrequently did the Ku Klux Klan march across the black campus or into the black community.

[3] Charles G. Gomillion, "The Tuskegee Voting Story," *Freedomways*, Vol. 2, No. 3 (Summer, 1962), p. 232.

Only infrequently did one hear of the white sheriff mistreating blacks—and then it was the "rural blacks," out on the plantations. Seldom, if ever, were "the Institute or hospital Negroes" mistreated. This, too, was part of the bargain.

Unlike other areas, also, the blacks in Tuskegee were not economically dependent upon the whites. There was no discernible way the local whites could invoke economic reprisals against black individuals as they could in Lowndes County, since many of the blacks were employed by the federal hospital and the private college. It was among these blacks that the leadership of the black community centered. Let us take a closer look at the structure of Tuskegee's "Negro Establishment."

The people in the top echelons of the college and the hospital were powerful in the black community because they could exact certain very limited benefits from the white power structure (a traffic light at a certain corner, a paved road) here and there. They were also influential in the black community because the middle-class blacks identified with them. The rural black people either did not matter or they looked up to the "Institute colored folks" —a logical carry-over from the days when Booker T. Washington and his assistants maintained a close, paternalistic relationship with the black people in the outlying areas. The distinctions between power and influence which existed in Lowndes County did not exist in Macon. The black ministry was not nearly as influential in Tuskegee as in, say, Lowndes. In later years—the late fifties and sixties—ministers held a few leadership positions in the TCA (one was elected to the City Council and another to the county Board of Revenue in 1964), but positions of power or influence, or both, were generally held by the hospital staff and by Institute faculty members. As Professors Lewis Jones and Stanley Smith, two black sociologists on the Institute faculty in the late fifties, commented:

. . . the Negro ministers are not accorded the status and
recognition which they usually experience in other Deep
South communities. This may be explained, partially, by
the fact that they are lost in "a sea of professionals." [4]

No one in the black community challenged the established black leadership. Even the small group of people
who formed and developed the Tuskegee Civic Association
did not see themselves as striving to replace the traditional
leadership. The TCA was heavily oriented toward education: toward a program of careful, patient study of such
things as the duties of local county officers, the duties of
citizenship, etc. In a sense, they were simply extending the
curriculum outlined by Booker T. Washington to include
civic concern. Professor Gomillion has written:

> The officers of the TCA have considered their major respon-
> sibility to be that of the civic education of all citizens in the
> community, Negro and white, and the facilitation of intelli-
> gent civic action on the part of an increasing number of
> Negro citizens.[5]

The black leadership of the TCA never envisioned a
future which might include the formation of a separate
political party; they wanted, ultimately, to get within the
local Democratic party. That leadership did not perceive
itself as out to overthrow, replace or supplement established
structures, much less alter the system. That leadership was
never alienated from the established values of the society;
they believed it was possible to work within the existing
structures to bring about change. Thus, the TCA could gain
the allegiance of many blacks in the community without
those blacks seeing themselves as turning their backs on
their philosophical leader, Booker T. Washington. Again
in the spirit of Washington, the black people of Tuskegee

---

[4] Lewis Jones and Stanley Smith, *Voting Rights and Economic Pressure*,
Anti-Defamation League, 1958, p. x.

[5] Gomillion, *op. cit.*, p. 233.

told themselves that they could convert their white neighbors, that they could "work with" the whites in town—at first, economically, and then, hopefully, politically.

The TCA held a peculiar position in the black community. Not many people openly supported it (and many wished it would just quiet down), but they recognized that something was wrong with the one-way deferential relationship existing between the races in the community. They knew that it was incongruous for them to have economic and educational achievements and to remain at the political mercy of a white minority. It was, to say the least, embarrassing, and for this reason many black people never talked about it. They withdrew and let the TCA fight their political battles. So the Institute administration affirmed its position on academic freedom, that it would not censure the civic acts of its professors (this affirmation went only so far, however), while the federal hospital kept one eye on its employees and the other on the Hatch Act, which prohibited "partisan political" activity by governmental workers.

Naturally the middle-class blacks of Tuskegee would have preferred to vote and be a part of political decision-making, but they needed a potent catalyst to spring them into action. Apparently, they still believed that they had not proven themselves enough in the Washington sense; indeed, they were—and in many respects, remain—like little children constantly looking for love from their parents—an approving pat on the head, a condescending smile—despite the fact that those parents are derelict, neglectful, even vicious to them.

One jolt came in 1957.

It had become clear by then that blacks in Macon County would soon have more votes than the whites. Although the TCA leadership had been making conciliatory statements for years to the effect that "We do not intend to take over complete power," the whites of the county and the state were not reassured. They did not believe them because it was unnatural *not* to vote against those who had kept you in political subordination for decades. The whites assumed that the blacks would recognize that their political interest required them—in the context of twentieth-century Macon County history—to vote for black people. What white person had not participated in the racist past, and whose sincerity would be trusted now? The whites therefore persuaded the state legislature to pass a law gerrymandering the city of Tuskegee. On July 13, 1957, the city boundaries were changed to make a four-sided municipality into a 28-sided one. Some 420 black voters were thereby excluded from the city; ten black voters were left; no whites were touched. The growing black vote could not take control of the city. This was Alabama's answer to the teachings of "political patience" of Booker T. Washington.

As Professor Lewis Jones has said, the whites breached the contract between Booker T. and the white community. Washington had understood that "eventually" the blacks would be permitted entrance into the political arena, but the whites had "never" in their minds. The middle-class blacks were shocked and hurt; they could not believe that their good white neighbors would do this to them! The TCA called for a selective-buying campaign (boycotts were illegal under the state law) against the white merchants in the town. They assumed that the law would not have been passed without the consent—tacit or overt—of the city. (This, again, points to the black community's strongly held view, nationwide, that a monolithic white power structure exists.)

The "boycott" lasted for about four years at a high level of effectiveness. During a period of two years, twenty-six businesses operated by whites closed down. But even then, the whites did not give in politically. The black people of Tuskegee had economic independence from local whites and they used it. But their *political* power did not increase.

Apparently, the whites were willing to suffer economic disaster rather then concede political power to the blacks. (The city boundaries were not restored until 1961, and then as a result of legal action culminating in a federal court decision of 1961 which ruled that the gerrymander had been racially motivated in violation of the Fifteenth Amendment and that a state may not gerrymander municipal boundaries on the basis of race. The former boundaries were restored.)[6]

Writing in 1958, Jones and Smith declared:

> The application of economic pressure by Negroes in withholding trade from white merchants has seriously endangered the business community and has created an economic crisis for the entire area. However, since the application of such pressure was designed to influence and change the political attitude of merchants and other white groups toward Negro voting rights, it is necessary to observe that the goal of the Negro campaign has not been achieved. . . . Historically, it is significant that in this major test, the dominant white group has been economically affected to a very serious degree by Negro action, though its political power remains intact.[7]

The blacks had achieved education and economic security —both of which are still projected throughout the nation as cure-alls—but the whites continued to lay and collect taxes, rule over the school system, determine law enforcement practices. The reason is obvious enough: blacks did not have *political* power. Economic security or the promise of it may, as we noted in Chapter V, be vital to the building of a strong political force. But in a vacuum it is of no use to black people working for meaningful change.

[6] The gerrymander case went up to the Supreme Court, which made the crucial procedural ruling that a federal court could hear the case. The whites had argued that the issue was political, not juridical. Once referred to a federal court, Judge Frank M. Johnson ruled in favor of the black appellants.

[7] Jones and Smith, *op. cit.*, p. 43.

During the same period as the gerrymander dispute, the United States Commission on Civil Rights conducted investigations in Macon County, which highlighted the long-term denial of voting rights. TCA officials testified before the Commission and were able to show that during the seven-year period from 1951 to 1958, 1,585 applications for voter certificates were made by blacks. Only 510 certificates were issued. The TCA documented that, for a twelve and one-half year period prior to December 1, 1958, Macon County was without a Board of Registrars for a total of three years and four months as a result of resignations and the refusal of the Governor and other members of the state appointing board to fill vacancies. Of course, the Governor refused to appoint any black people to the Board of Registrars. The picture presented to the Commission was one of continuous political frustration of black efforts.

The TCA demonstrated great skill in administration and data-collecting—a skill which defies the claim of some whites and blacks in the community that black people would not be able to run the county and city governmental machinery. The TCA produced a complete record of every black person who applied for a voter certificate since 1951, the number admitted into the registration office and the length of time needed for each to complete the application process. A TCA representative was stationed at the court-house day after day, year after year—how patient can black folks be?—to record this information; that person also noted the time the Board of Registrars started work, the length of time it remained in session, and the days it was supposed to meet but did not do so.

As if to add further white insult to black injury, the TCA had documented that it could not receive a hearing from the person allegedly representing Macon County in the state legislature. In Feburary, 1959, the TCA sent him a certified letter; it was *returned, unopened, marked "Refused"!* And all this in a county where black people had a majority, were economically independent and were educated. Yet the country never seemed to get too upset about White Power.

In 1959, Macon County became one of the first counties against which the Department of Justice filed a suit charging voting denials. Slowly, tediously, with one judicial decree after another handed down by federal Judge Frank M. Johnson, sitting in Montgomery, black people were added to the rolls. Soon the number of blacks exceeded whites as voters by a substantial margin. In 1964, there were approximately 7,212 voters in the county: 3,733 blacks, 3,479 whites. In 1966, these figures had increased substantially: 6,803 blacks, 4,495 whites. The white fears which had instigated the attempted gerrymander came true.

Now the big question was: would black people run for office and attempt to take and use political power? New groups and individuals in the community began to urge that blacks vote for blacks. But the TCA was true to its word: it decided in 1964 not to contest all five seats on the City Council; to run no black person for the powerful position of probate judge; to endorse only one black person for the county Board of Revenue.

These decisions were made on the premises that (1) it was wiser to seek only a few offices in order to show the local whites that they had nothing to fear from the growing black vote; (2) it was best to gain "experience" in public office before even thinking about assuming full control; (3) if the blacks elected all black candidates, the whites—in addition to pulling up stakes and leaving the county—might, during the lame-duck period, so disrupt the financial status of the county as to render the incoming blacks incapable of governing effectively.

A new group of black people in the community, the Non-Partisan Voters' League, took strong exception to this position. They felt that the least the black people should do was to control a majority of the seats on the City

Council and on the county Board of Revenue, in addition to electing a black probate judge.

The TCA leadership counseled black people to vote a straight Democratic party ticket: a slate of black and white candidates, who were endorsed by the Macon County Democratic Club, the political arm of the TCA. They counseled black people *not* to vote for the independent black candidates endorsed by the Non-Partisan Voters' League. In a statement to the black leaders of the county precincts, dated October 28, 1964, Gomillion said:

Dear Leaders in the Precincts:

Following is a statement which might be used as a guide for your thinking and for the information which you give to voters on Monday evening, November 2, when you meet with them.

1. The Macon County Democratic Club officers believe:

   a. That Negro voters can demonstrate political strength and power most effectively by affiliation with, and participation in, a political party.

   b. That such political power by Macon County Negroes can best be expressed through the Democratic Party, at least at the present time.

   c. That the best way to reveal or express that power in the election of November 3 is by casting the largest possible number of votes for the *Democratic nominees*.

   d. That the best way to cast the largest number of votes is by voting the *straight Democratic ticket*.

   . . . .

   h. That voting the straight Democratic ticket on November 3 might give the impression that we *know* what we want, and we know *how* to get it.

   . . . .

   j. That voting the straight Democratic ticket for *all* Democratic nominees on state and county levels will reveal to us the kind of strength available for possible use in electing other Negroes to positions in the County, such as tax collector, members of the County Democratic

Committee, members of the Lower House of the Alabama Legislature.

. . . The important issue here is whether or not we want to continue to act and be treated as Negroes, or to move into the larger area of politics and act as Democrats, who *happen* to be Negroes. . . . The Club did *not* refrain from endorsing the Independents because they are Negroes, but because they are Independents. . . . Let's show Alabama and the Democratic National Committee that Macon County Negro voters are loyal Democrats.

The TCA/MCDC position carried the day. The white press around the country praised the black people of Tuskegee for their decision not to take over all the offices, for not pre-empting all the public offices, for not establishing a "black oligarchy" to replace a "white oligarchy." Tuskegee blacks were showing "good sense," "forbearance." The country began to look upon Tuskegee once again as a "model" for other racially tense areas; it was pointing the way for other black people. Tuskegee was thus launched on a new political experiment—"bi-racial" government in the black-belt South. A novel thing indeed!

The two black people elected to the Tuskegee City Council immediately came in for severe criticism from a portion of the black community. The councilmen were criticized for not speaking out more for the black race, for not raising the issue of segregation in some white-owned places. The important and curious thing about these complaints was that since ultimate power still remained with the whites, the *only* thing the two token councilmen could do was "speak out." This did not, of course, mean that the grievances would be alleviated. With the existing ratio of 3–2 on the Council, the blacks could still be out-voted. The pitiful thing is that the black community had not needed to settle for representatives who could only "speak out"; it could have had political control.

Complaints were also heard against the white mayor for

not appointing a black person to serve as clerk in the city office; political threats had to be made before he relented. Two black people were elected as justices of the peace, but the white sheriff did not take business to them.

In 1966, Tuskegee got a second jolt.

During the summer of the previous year, a number of Tuskegee Institute students had challenged various forms of overt discrimination which existed in the town. They had tried to enter "white" restaurants (and had been refused), held rallies, picketed stores for not hiring black people. Several times they tried to attend the segregated white churches, and were brutally beaten twice. Then, in January of 1966, one of the student leaders—Sammy Younge, Jr.— was shot to death by a white man when he sought to use the "white" rest-room at a gas station. (The man was later acquitted by an all-white jury in another county.) Younge himself was a member of a respected middle-class family in the town; his murder (not to mention the beatings at the churches) should have made clear to the black middle-class the folly and hopelessness of their previous approach. For some, it did; others went their comfortable way, unchanged.

Later that year, with no encouragement or aid from the TCA, a black citizen, Lucius Amerson, decided to run for sheriff of the county. One officer of the TCA—himself a member of the City Council—came out publicly in favor of the incumbent white sheriff as "the better man." Amerson waged a campaign throughout the county, especially among the rural black people. It was not a "racist" campaign; time and again he reiterated that he would conduct his office equitably and without favoritism to race. Amerson was elected in November, 1966, despite the lack of TCA support.

But the White Power of the community lingered on. Amerson was immediately faced with efforts by the whites to undercut his power. The white-controlled Board of Revenue reappointed the outgoing sheriff as Beer License

Inspector, a position Amerson stated he wanted inasmuch as his duties included such matters. The Board denied him extra funds needed to operate his office. White constables were appointed by the local white justices of the peace in an attempt to circumvent the new sheriff's law enforcement power.

In other areas of Tuskegee life, whites retained ultimate control in 1967. The City Council remains controlled by whites; so does the county Board of Revenue, the school board, the offices of probate judge, tax assessor, county solicitor and several local planning boards.

There are several conclusions one could draw about this county in black-belt Alabama.

1) The middle-class black community is clinging to a set of values and a rhetoric which never applied in that area or any other of this country: a language of Christian love, charity, good will. When Sammy Younge, Jr. was killed, a frustrated student group held protest demonstrations in the town, and there was some damage to property as a result of the demonstrators being harassed and intimidated by local police. Vocal black people condemned the students rather than the conditions which permitted Younge to die. One Negro woman, prominent in civic affairs in Tuskegee, said:

Anyone who knows me understands that I yield to no one in dedication to equal citizenship rights. I have long worked for elimination of injustices and discrimination. I believe in the American dream—the Christian principle—of democracy for all regardless of race, color or creed. I have stood by this conviction.

In recent days, especially last Saturday, the events connected with the equal rights movement did nothing for progress but only damaged the cause of responsible citizenship. I refer, of course, to the display of undisciplined and irresponsible behavior by a few young persons which was marked by rock and bottle throwing. I am ashamed of every person

who set off this ugly incident or who had any part in it.
. . . the vast majority of mature, Christian, right-thinking
Negro citizens regret what happened.

There are many needs in the present situation. The first
is responsible action and the exercise of calm judgment by
every citizen. Those of us who live here and love this community have much at stake. The SNCC-type from outside
and the handful who are persuaded to act outside the law
do not seem to understand this. We want a type of relationship, built on solid ground, which will endure through the
years—a relationship depending upon mutual trust and respect. This does not derive from rowdyism and lawlessness.
. . . There was an article in last week's *Time* magazine
which referred to the recent inexcusable murder as having
removed the façade which had covered up lack of progress
in equal rights. Anyone who knew the voter situation here
several years ago and who knows the facts today could not
agree with that statement. . . . Sure, we have not realized
all our ambitions. Certainly, we have a long way to go. But
the important thing is that we were on the way—that we
had made remarkable progress, and that this progress had
been made without violence of any type.

. . . Tuskegee is our home, we are proud of its institutions.
We insist on equality of opportunity—under law and under
God—but we are not radical street demonstrators, losing control of our good instincts. Nor will we endorse or support
those who work without purpose or concern for law and
order.

Let all of us—white and colored—join hands in securing
justice, obedience to law and good will which will bring
progress in every area of our common life.[8]

This letter represents the thinking of a vast number of
middle-class black people in Tuskegee. These people do, in
fact, "believe in the American dream." But that dream, as
already noted, was not originally intended to include them
and it does not include the black masses today.

[8] Letter to the Editor, *The Tuskegee News* (January 20, 1966), p. 2.

Nor is the lady realistic about white attitudes. Black people must stop deluding themselves that the basic intentions of *most* white people are good. White America, in many ways, has been telling black people that the hopes and language of the letter reproduced above are nothing more than naïve lamentations. Note the warnings of the "respectable" editorial writers of *The Saturday Evening Post*:

> We are all, let us face it, Mississippians. We all fervently wish that the Negro problem did not exist, or that, if it must exist, it could be ignored. Confronted with the howling need for decent schools, jobs, housing, and all the other minimum rights of the American system, we will do our best, in a half-hearted way, to correct old wrongs. The hand may be extended grudgingly and patronizingly, but anyone who rejects that hand rejects his own best interests. *For minimum rights are the only rights that we are willing to guarantee, and above those minimum rights there is and will continue to be a vast area of discrimination and inequity and unfairness,* the area in which we claim the most basic right of all—the right to be stupid and prejudiced, the right to make mistakes, the right to be less and worse than we pretend, the right to be ourselves.[9] (Authors' italics).

These clear indications of feelings make the language of Tuskegee's middle-class black people seem ludicrous—and also rather shameful. Such blacks are pleased that certain changes have occurred without violence. But had there been a more sincere confrontation with whites by those blacks so intent on avoiding violence for avoidance's sake, Sammy Younge and many other black people would not be dead today. Those who look to Tuskegee for progress should ponder the following statement of a professor on the faculty at the Institute:

[9] "A New White Backlash?" *The Saturday Evening Post* (September 10, 1966), p. 88.

If one considers Tuskegee to be a model community that has made steady progress toward racial reconciliation rooted in mutual respect and acceptance, it is difficult to explain the intense reaction to Younge's death—an intensity that is only weakly suggested by the four civil rights marches that have already occurred. In point of fact, the events of the past year make it abundantly clear that Tuskegee has been living a lie—a lie made all the more dangerous by the apparent control that Negroes have secured over the political agencies of the community. . . . The fault lies in the self-deceptive nature of the vision that guides both groups, and in the external pressure that constrains that vision from moving from status to contract.[10]

The black people of Tuskegee—the largely middle-class blacks—soothe themselves into thinking that they are describing what is or can be. They are simply deceiving themselves. Their grand language—applauded by many whites—may make them feel morally superior but it does nothing to gain political power, the power necessary to stop killings and discrimination. Black people of Tuskegee do not need to show whites that they can talk a good rhetoric. White people know that power is not love, Christian charity, etc. If these things come, let them develop out of a respect for mutual power. The whites will stop killing blacks and kidding blacks when the blacks make it no longer worthwhile for them to do so.

The black people of Tuskegee are perpetuating a deferential society wherein the blacks must always prove something to the whites. First, they had to prove that they could wash up, clean up, get an education and be nice little black people before the whites would "accept" them. Then, when they got the ballot—with absolutely no help from the local whites—they had to prove their patience and

---

[10] Arnold S. Kaufman, "Murder in Tuskegee: Day of Wrath in the Model Town," *The Nation* (January 31, 1966), p. 119.

good will by not making effective use of it. Supposedly, they had to learn how to govern from the white man. No more succinct rejection of this view has been articulated than that of Dr. Paul L. Puryear, formerly of the Tuskegee faculty: "How can we learn from those who have demonstrated their incompetence?"

The whites of Tuskegee have ruled for decades and that rule has been despotic. The only lesson the whites of Tuskegee could teach the black people was how to exclude blacks from positions of power. Black people must not indulge the fanciful notion that whites, because they are white, have a priority on leadership talent. The only sure talent that Tuskegee whites have demonstrated is the ability to suppress and oppress black people. To cater to this despicable history in the name of "love" and "bi-racialism" is absurd. The black people should create rather than imitate—create new forms which are politically inclusive rather than imitate old racist forms which are politically exclusive. The black people have nothing to prove to the whites; the burden is on the whites to prove that they are civilized enough to live in the community and to share in its governance.

Tuskegee, Alabama, could be the model of Black Power. It could be the place where black people have amassed political power and used that power effectively. The black people of Tuskegee could play a major role in building an independent county political organization which would address itself to the needs of black residents along lines we have already indicated. Such an independent force would give greater meaning to the election of Amerson by creating a genuine, organized base of power—not merely putting one black man, however valuable, into office. In addition, despite the special circumstances prevailing in Macon County—the high educational level, economic security—Tuskegee Institute could serve as a training center for potential indigenous community leaders from other areas.

It would be naïve to expect that the operation of Black Power in Tuskegee could transform Alabama state politics. But it could establish in that one area a viable government based on a new and different set of values—on humaneness —and serve as an example of what civilized government *could* be in this society.

Black people need not be apologetic or defensive about controlling their communities in this manner. We have seen that this is the one sure way to end racism in this country. The Tuskegee model *could* be applicable to black areas in other parts of the country, including the northern ghettos. Although no widespread possibility of governing whole counties exists in the North at this time, we are aware that, in the very near future, many of the northern urban cities will be predominantly black. Pockets of Black Power could develop and become illustrations of what *legitimate* government really is—a phenomenon we have not experienced to date in this society. In the next two chapters we will take a look at the urban ghettos and some possible forms for giving substance to our goals.

C H A P T E R | V I I

DYNAMITE

❶ This country is known by its cities: those amazing aggregations of people and housing, offices and factories, which constitute the heart of our civilization, the nerve center of our collective being. America is increasingly dominated by her cities, as they draw into them the brawn and brains and wealth of the hinterland. Seventy percent of the American people now reside in urban areas—all of which are in a state of crisis. It is estimated that by 1980, an additional fifty-three million people will be living in the cities. By 2000, ninety-five percent of all Americans will be living in urban areas.[1] Millions of these will be black people. For a number of reasons, the city has become the major

[1] *Congressional Record*, January 23, 1967.

in the Ghetto

domestic problem facing this nation in the second half of the twentieth century.

Corporate power has moved its structure and influence to the cities. . . . No longer do public land grabs and privileged tax structures suffice for corporate power. Instead, they require centralization, intellect and skill for the administration of its productive technology. For these and other reasons, the corporation has come full force to the city. Their procession requires favorable opinion to withstand public misgiving. Thus, they have come to control the media, the schools, the press, the university—either by way of ownership, contract, or public service. . . .

Federalism is also moving to the city, through the growth of direct federal-local relations in education, housing, transportation, public welfare, etc. A nation of urban federalism is emerging, while the states gradually become regional administrations of the national government. . . .

Its major interest formation is the new middle class. Technology, corporate consolidation, and public economy are transforming that class from a property to a wage base. It is a college-educated class of salaried administrators, whose primary interest is to secure more objects for service, management, and control. For this purpose the middle class needs a permanently expanding dependent clientele and enough organizational power to protect its function and expanding ranks. Service and expertise are its occupational principles. So the new class seeks to enlarge service programs; refine the qualifications of performance; and control their operation through professional organization. . . .

Correspondingly, the lower class has been transformed from production to permanent unemployment. Its value is no longer labor, but dependency. . . . Both groups and allied interests are in daily battle, which is manifested in the recurring disorders that surround housing, education, and welfare administration. . . .

The crucial issue of the public control of technology rests in the city. Here the felt effects of technology meet the popular power to question, resist, and even possibly, to democratically guide automation to better purpose. Whether democratic decision can prevail over the private control of technology is questionable. But the issue will have to be met in the city.[2]

[2] Milton Kotler, *Community Foundation Memorandum No. 6, The Urban Polity:* remarks introducing a staff discussion on community foundations at the Center for the Study of Democratic Institutions, Santa Barbara, California, January 8, 1965.

The problems of the city and of institutional racism are clearly intertwined. Nowhere are people so expendable in the forward march of corporate power as in the ghetto. At the same time, nowhere is the potential political power of black people greater. If the crisis we face in the city is to be dealt with, the problem of the ghetto must be solved first.

Black people now hold the balance of electoral power in some of the nation's largest cities, while population experts predict that, in the next ten to twenty years, black Americans will constitute the majority in a dozen or more of the largest cities. In Washington, D.C., and Newark, New Jersey, they already are in the majority; in Detroit, Baltimore, Cleveland and St. Louis, they represent one-third or slightly more of the population; in such places as Oakland, Chicago, Philadelphia and Cincinnati, they constitute well over one-fourth. Even at the height of European immigration, no ethnic group has ever multiplied so rapidly in the United States. In order to understand the black ghetto —both its great problems and its capacity to become a key political force in urban America—we should take a brief look at the history of black migration to the North.

■

Many slaves escaped to the North before emancipation, while some, of course, migrated to Liberia, Haiti and Central America. The Emancipation Proclamation cut many loose from the land and, starting with the end of the Civil War, there developed a steady trickle of freed men from the South. During Reconstruction, this northward migration eased somewhat with the ability of black people to take advantage of the franchise.

Soon after, however, southern racism and fanaticism broke loose. Thousands of black people were killed in the 1870's in an effort by whites to destroy the political power that blacks had gained. This was all capped by the deal of

1876 (mentioned in Chapter IV), whereby the Republicans guaranteed that Mr. Hayes, when he became President, would, by non-interference and the withdrawal of troops, allow the planters—under the name of Democrats —to gain control in the Deep South. The withdrawal of these troops by President Hayes and the appointment of a Kentuckian and a Georgian to the Supreme Court marked the handwriting on the wall.

In *Black Reconstruction*, DuBois portrays the situation clearly:

> Negroes did not surrender the ballot easily or immediately. They continued to hold remnants of political power in South Carolina, Florida, Louisiana, in parts of North Carolina, Texas, Tennessee and Virginia. Black Congressmen came out of the South until 1895 and Black legislators served as late as 1896. But in a losing battle with public opinion, industry and wealth against them . . . the decisive influence was the systematic and overwhelming economic pressure. Negroes who wanted work must not dabble in politics. . . . From 1880 onward, in order to earn a living, the American Negro was compelled to give up his political power [pp. 692–93].

Black people were therefore looking to move again. About 60,000 went to Kansas, two-thirds of them destitute on arrival. In general, however, migration to escape the new regime in the South did not really get under way until World War I. Business was booming in 1914–15 as this nation became a major supplier of war materials to the Allies. This in turn increased the job market and, with the war cutting off the flow of immigrants from Europe, northern industry went on a massive campaign to recruit black workers. Emigration from the Deep South jumped from 200,000 in the decade 1890–1900 to half a million in 1910–1920. This migration northward did not cease with the conclusion of the war. The Immigration and Exclusion Acts of the early twenties created a great demand by industry for more workers (especially with the new assembly-line concept employed by Ford). As a result, during the twenties and thirties about 1,300,000 black people migrated from the Deep South to the North. By 1940, over 2,000,-000 blacks had migrated northward. (However, as late as 1940 more than three out of every four black people still remained in the South.)

World War II intensified black migration out of the Deep South, more so than World War I had done. Black people moved to Los Angeles, Pittsburgh, Akron, Gary, Kansas City, Cincinnati, Philadelphia, Washington, Chicago, New York and many other places. They found work in the steel mills, aircraft factories and shipyards as, for the most part, laborers and domestics. During the forties, roughly 250,000 blacks migrated to the West Coast alone to find work. This migration did not slow down with the end of the war but continued into the sixties.

The United States Census indicates:

Rise in Black Population Outside South

	% of Total	No. of Blacks
1900	10	1,647,377
1910	11	1,899,654
1920	15	2,407,371
1930	21	3,483,746
1940	23	3,986,606
1950	32	5,989,543
1960	40	9,009,470

Today, over sixty-five percent of black people live in urban America. This figure, of course, includes many of the urban areas of the South—Atlanta, Birmingham, Jackson, etc. Mechanization of southern plantations has been a major reason for the migration. In 1966, over seventy-five percent of all cotton was picked by machines in the seventeen major cotton-growing counties of Mississippi. (A machine can pick one bale of cotton per hour; it takes an able-bodied man one week to pick a bale.)

Census data tell us that the largest percentage increase in black population was in the West, especially California. About 8 percent of the black population lived in the West in 1966, compared with 5.7 percent in 1960. Increases in the Northeast and North Central states were not as sharp, although the overall percentages were greater. (17.9 percent of the black population lived in the Northeast in 1966, compared with 16 percent in 1960, while 20.2 percent lived in the North Central states compared with 18.3 percent in 1960.)

What problems did black people face as they moved into these areas? Most of the blacks moving to the North were crowded into the slums of the cities. In the face of bombs and riots, they fought for a place to live and room for relatives and friends who followed them. They also faced a daily fight for jobs. At first, they were refused industrial employment and forced to accept menial work. As we have seen, wartime brought many jobs, but during periods of recession and depression blacks were the first cut from the job market while skill and craft jobs for the most part remained closed to them. Added to the problems of housing and jobs, of course, was that of education. By the early part of the twentieth century, these three issues had become fundamental problems of the ghetto and fundamental issues in the early racial explosions. The city of Chicago offers a classic illustration of this type.

As black people started arriving in Chicago at the turn of the century, they were forced into old ghettos, where rents were cheapest and housing poorest. They took over the old, dilapidated shacks near the railroad tracks—and close to the vice areas. The tremendous demand for housing resulted in an immediate skyrocketing of rents in the ghetto. Artificial panics were often created by enterprising realtors who raised the cry: "The niggers are coming," and then proceeded to double the rents after the whites had fled.

The expansion of the ghetto developed so much friction that bombs were often thrown at black-owned homes in the expanding neighborhoods. In Chicago, over a dozen black homes were bombed between July 1, 1917, and July 1, 1919. This sporadic bombing of black homes was but the prelude to a five-day riot in July, 1919, which took at least thirty-eight lives, resulted in over five hundred injuries, destroyed $250,000 worth of property, and left over a thousand persons homeless. In their book, *Black Metropolis*, St. Clair Drake and Horace Cayton describe how the riot was ended on the sixth day by the state militia, belatedly called after the police had shown their inability and, in some instances, their unwillingness, to curb attacks on black people (p. 64).

A non-partisan, interracial Chicago Commission on Race Relations was appointed to investigate and to make recommendations. According to Drake and Cayton, the Comission recommended the correction of gross inequities in protection on the part of the police and the state's attorney; it also rebuked the courts for facetiousness in dealing with black defendants and the police for discrimination in making arrests. The Board of Education was asked to exercise special care in selecting principals and teachers in ghetto schools (schools at that time were segregated by law, or *de jure*, while today ghetto schools are segregated *de facto*), to alleviate overcrowding and double-shift schools. Employers and labor organizations were admonished in some detail against the use of black workers as strikebreakers and against excluding them from unions and industries. The City Council was asked to condemn all houses unfit for human habitation, of which the Commission found many in the black ghetto. The Commission also affirmed the rights of black people to live anywhere they wanted and could afford to live in the city. It insisted that property depreciation in black areas was often due to factors other than black occupancy; it condemned arbitrary increase of rents and designated the amounts and quality of housing as an all-important factor in Chicago's race problem. Looking at these recommendations, we realized that they are not only similar but almost identical to the demands made by Dr. Martin Luther King's group forty-seven years later in Chicago—not to mention other urban areas in the 1960's.

Such explosions and recommendations were to be heard many more times in urban areas all over the country during the twenties, thirties and forties. But in the fifties a political protest movement was born which had a calming, wait-and-see effect on the attitude of many urban black people. There was the Supreme Court decision of 1954; the Montgomery bus boycott of '55–'57; the dispatch of federal troops to Little Rock, Arkansas, to prevent interference with school desegregation in '57. The student sit-in movement in '60 and '61, the emotional appeal of President Kennedy and the great amount of visibility given to the NAACP, Urban League, CORE, SNCC and other civil rights organizations further contributed to creating a period of relative calm in the ghetto.

Then, in the spring of 1963, the lull was over.

The eruption in Birmingham, Alabama, in the spring of 1963 showed how quickly anger can develop into violence. Black people were angry about the killing of Emmett Till and Charles Mack Parker; the failure of federal, state and city governments to deal honestly with the problems of ghetto life. Now they read in the newspapers, saw on television and watched from the street corners themselves the police dogs and the fire hoses and the policemen beating their friends and relatives. They watched as young high-school students and women were beaten, as Martin Luther King and his co-workers were marched off to jail. The spark was ignited when a black-owned motel in Birmingham and the home of Dr. King's brother were bombed. This incident brought hundreds of angry black people into the street throwing rocks and bottles and sniping at policemen. The echoes were far and wide. In Chicago, a few days later, two black youths assaulted the mayor's eighteen-year-old nephew, shouting: "This is for Birmingham." It was for Birmingham, true, but it was for three hundred and fifty years of history before Birmingham as well. The explosions were soon to be heard in Harlem, Chicago, Philadelphia and Rochester in '64, Watts in '65, Omaha, Atlanta, Dayton and dozens of other places in '66. James Baldwin stated it clearly in 1963: "When a race riot occurs . . . it will not spread merely to Birmingham. . . . The trouble will spread to every metropolitan center in the nation which has a significant Negro population."

This brief scan of history clearly indicates that the disturbances in our cities are not just isolated reactions to the cry of "Black Power," but part of a pattern. The problems of Harlem in the 1960's are not much different from those of Harlem in 1920.

■

The core problem within the ghetto is the vicious circle created by the lack of decent housing, decent jobs and adequate education. The failure of these three fundamental institutions to work has led to alienation of the ghetto from the rest of the urban area as well as to deep political rifts between the two communities.

In America we judge by American standards, and by this yardstick we find that the black man lives in incredibly inadequate housing, shabby shelters that are dangerous to mental and physical health and to life itself. It has been estimated that twenty million black people put fifteen billion dollars into rents, mortgage payments and housing expenses every year. But because his choice is largely limited to the ghettos, and because the black population is increasing at a rate which is 150 percent over that of the increase in the white population, the shelter shortage for the black person is not only acute and perennial, but getting increasingly tighter. Black people are automatically forced to pay top dollar for whatever they get, even a 6 x 6 cold-water flat.

Urban renewal and highway clearance programs have forced black people more and more into congested pockets of the inner city. Since suburban zoning laws have kept out low-income housing, and the Federal Government has failed to pass open-occupancy laws, black people are forced to stay in the deteriorating ghettos. Thus crowding increases, and slum conditions worsen.

In the Mill Creek (East St. Louis), Illinois, urban renewal undertaking, for instance, a black slum was cleared and in its place rose a middle-income housing development. What happened to those evicted to make way for this great advance? The majority were forced into what remained of the black ghetto; in other words, the crowding was intensified.

Here we begin to understand the pervasive, cyclic implications of institutional racism. Barred from most housing, black people are forced to live in segregated neighborhoods and with this comes de facto segregated schooling, which means poor education, which leads in turn to ill-paying jobs.

It is impossible to talk about the problems of education in the black community without at some point dealing with the issue of desegregation and integration, especially since the Supreme Court decision of May 17, 1954: " . . . In the field of public education the doctrine of separate but equal has no place. Separate education facilities are inherently unequal." However, all the discussion of integration or bussing today seems highly irrelevant; it allows a lot of highly paid school administrators to talk around and never deal with the problem. For example, in Washington, D.C., the schools were supposedly integrated immediately after the 1954 decision, but as a result of the population movements of whites into suburbs and blacks into the inner (ghetto) city, black children attend what are in fact segregated schools. Today, roughly 85 percent of the children in the Washington, D.C. public schools are black. Nor is integration very relevant or meaningful in any of the other major urban areas. In Chicago, 87 percent of the black students in elementary school attend virtually all-black public schools. In Detroit, 45 percent of the black students are in public schools that are overwhelmingly black. In Philadelphia, thirty-eight elementary schools have a black enrollment of 99 percent. In April, 1967, the Rev. Henry Nichols, vice president of the Philadelphia School Board, stated on television that that the city had two separate school systems: one for the ghetto, the other for the rest of the city. There was no public denial from any other knowledgeable sources in the city. In Los Angeles, forty-three elementary schools have at least 85 percent black attendance. In the Borough of Manhattan in New York City, 77 percent of the elementary school students and 72 percent of the junior high school students are black.[3]

Clearly, "integration"—even if it would solve the educational problem—has not proved feasible. The alternative presented is usually the large-scale transfer of black children to schools in white neighborhoods. This too raises several problems, already mentioned in Chapter II. Implicit is the idea that the closer you get to whiteness, the better you are. Another problem is that it makes the majority of black youth expendable. Probably the maximum number of blacks who could transfer from ghetto schools to white schools, given the overcrowded conditions of city schools anyway, is about 20 percent. The 80 percent left behind are therefore expendable.

The real need at present is not integration but quality education.

[3] Tom Kahn, *The Economics of Equality*, League for Industrial Democracy, 1964, pp. 31–32.

In Central Harlem, for example, there are twenty elementary schools, four junior high schools and no high schools. A total of 31,469 students—virtually all black—attend these schools. In New York as a whole, only 50.3 percent of the teachers in the black and Puerto Rican elementary schools were fully licensed as compared with 78.2 percent in white schools.[4]

In 1960, in Central Harlem, 21.6 percent of third-grade students were reading above grade level and 30 percent were reading below. By the sixth grade, 11.7 percent are reading above and 80 percent are reading below grade level. The median equivalent grades reading comprehension for Central Harlem, third grade, was a full year behind the city median and the national norm, and by the sixth grade it was two years behind. The same is true of word knowledge. In arithmetic, the students of Central Harlem are one and a half years behind the rest of the city by the sixth grade, and by the time they are in the eighth grade, they are two years behind. The I. Q. scores are 90.6 in the third grade, and by the sixth grade they have gone down to 86.3.[5]

The basic story of education in Central Harlem emerges as one of inefficiency, inferiority and mass deterioration. It is a system which typifies colonialism and the colonist's attitude. Nor is Harlem unique. Rev. Henry Nichols, vice president of the Philadelphia Board of Education, stated in 1967 that 75 percent of the black children who would be graduated that year were "functional illiterates. . . . The reason for this," he added, "is the attitude of school administrators toward black people."[6]

There can be no doubt that in today's world a thorough

---

[4] *Ibid.*, p. 32.
[5] *Youth in the Ghetto*, New York: Harlem Youth Opportunities Unlimited (HARYOU), 1964, pp. 166–80.
[6] *The New York Times* (May 4, 1967), p. 23.

and comprehensive education is an absolute necessity. Yet it is obvious from the data that a not even minimum education is being received in most ghetto schools. White decision-makers have been running those schools with injustice, indifference and inadequacy for too long; the result has been an educationally crippled black child turned out onto the labor market equipped to do little more than stand in welfare lines to receive his miserable dole.

It should not be hard to understand why approximately 41 percent of the pupils entering high school from Central Harlem drop out before receiving a diploma, 52 percent of these being boys. When one couples school conditions with the overcrowded and deteriorating housing in which black pupils must live and study, additional factors become clear. Males, in particular, must leave school because of financial pressure. The young drop-out or even high school graduate with an inadequate education, burdened also by the emotional deprivations which are the consequences of poverty, is now on the street looking for a job.

The HARYOU report clearly states: "That the unemployment situation among Negro youth in Central Harlem is explosive can be readily seen in the fact that twice as many young Negroes in the labor force, as compared to their white counterparts, were without employment in 1960. For the girls the disparity was even greater: nearly two and one-half times the unemployment rate for white girls in the labor force. Undoubtedly this situation has worsened since 1960, in view of the report of the New York State Department of Labor indicating that job-hunting was generally tougher in 1963 than in the previous year. Also, it is generally conceded that official statistics on unemployment are considerably understated for black youth since only those persons actively looking for work in the past 60 days are included in census taking . . . such a situation building up, this mass of unemployed and frustrated Negro

youth, is social dynamite. We are presented with a phenomenon that may be compared with the piling up of in-
flammable material in an empty building in a city block." [7]

The struggle for employment has had a drastic effect on
the black community. It perpetuates the breakdown of the
black family structure. Many men who are unable to find
employment leave their homes so that their wives can
qualify for Aid to Dependent Children or welfare. Children growing up in a welfare situation often leave school
because of a lack of incentive or because they do not have
enough food to eat or clothes to wear. They in turn go out
to seek jobs but only find a more negative situation than
their fathers faced. So they turn to petty crime, pushing
dope, prostitution (joining the Army if possible), and the
cycle continues.

We have not touched on the issue of health and medical
care in the ghetto. Whitney Young documented conditions
at length in *To Be Equal;* the pattern is predictably dismal.
The black infant mortality rate in 1960 exceeded that in the
total population by 66 percent; the maternal death rate for
black women was four times as high as that for whites in
1960; the life expectancy for non-whites was six years less
than for whites; approximately 30 percent more white people have health insurance than blacks; only 2 percent of
the nation's physicians are black, which means that in
segregated areas one finds such situations as Mississippi
with a ratio of one doctor per 18,500 black residents!
Those of us who survive must indeed be a tough people.

■

These are the conditions which create dynamite in the
ghettos. And when there are explosions—explosions of
frustration, despair and hopelessness—the larger society becomes indignant and utters irrelevant clichés about maintaining law and order. Blue ribbon committees of "experts"

[7] *Youth in the Ghetto, op. cit.,* pp. 246–47.

and "consultants" are appointed to investigate the "causes of the riot." They then spend hundreds of thousands of dollars on preparing "authoritative" reports. Some token money from the Office of Economic Opportunity may be promised and then everybody either prays for rain to cool off tempers and vacate the streets or for an early autumn.

This country, with its pervasive institutional racism, has itself created socially undesirable conditions; it merely perpetuates those conditions when it lays the blame on people who, through whatever means at their disposal, seek to strike out at the conditions. What has to be understood is that thus far there have been virtually no *legitimate* programs to deal with the alienation and the oppressive conditions in the ghettos. On April 9, 1967, a few days after Mayor Daley won an overwhelming, unprecedented fourth-term victory (receiving, incidentally, approximately 85 percent of Chicago's black vote), *The New York Times* editorialized: "Like other big-city mayors, Mr. Daley has no long-range plans for coping with the social dislocation caused by the steady growth of the Negro population. He tries to manage the effects of that dislocation and hopes for the best."

Herein lies the match that will continue to ignite the dynamite in the ghettos: the ineptness of decision-makers, the anachronistic institutions, the inability to think boldly and above all the unwillingness to innovate. The make-shift plans put together every summer by city administrations to avoid rebellions in the ghettos are merely buying time. White America can continue to appropriate millions of dollars to take ghetto teen-agers off the streets and onto nice, green farms during the hot summer months. They can continue to provide mobile swimming pools and hastily built play areas, but there is a point beyond which the steaming ghettos will not be cooled off. It is ludicrous for the society to believe that these temporary measures can long contain the tempers of an oppressed people. And when the dynamite does go off, pious pronouncements of patience should not go forth. Blame should not be placed on "outside agitators" or on "Communist influence" or on advocates of Black Power. That dynamite was placed there by white racism and it was ignited by white racist indifference and unwillingness to act justly.

CHAPTER | VIII

THE SEARCH

○ We are aware that it has become commonplace to pinpoint and describe the ills of our urban ghettos. The social, political and economic problems are so acute that even a casual observer cannot fail to see that something is wrong. While description is plentiful, however, there remains a blatant timidity about what to *do* to solve the problems.

Neither rain nor endless "definitive," costly reports nor stop-gap measures will even approach a solution to the explosive situation in the nation's ghettos. This country cannot begin to solve the problems of the ghettos as long as it continues to hang on to outmoded structures and institu-

for New Forms

tions. A political party system that seeks only to "manage conflict" and hope for the best will not be able to serve a growing body of alienated black people. An educational system which, year after year, continues to cripple hundreds of thousands of black children must be replaced by wholly new mechanisms of control and management. We must begin to think and operate in terms of entirely new and substantially different forms of expression.

It is crystal clear that the initiative for such changes will have to come from the black community. We cannot expect white America to begin to move forcefully on these problems unless and until black America begins to move.

This means that black people must organize themselves without regard for what is traditionally acceptable, precisely because the traditional approaches have failed. It means that black people must make demands without regard to their initial "respectability," precisely because "respectable" demands have not been sufficient.

The northern urban ghettos are in many ways different from the black-belt South, but in neither area will substantial change come about until black people organize independently to exert power. As noted in earlier chapters, black people already have the voting potential to control the politics of entire southern counties. Given maximum registration of blacks, there are more than 110 counties where black people could outvote the white racists. These people should concentrate on forming independent political parties and not waste time trying to reform or convert the racist parties. In the North, it is no less important that independent groups be formed. It has been clearly shown that when black people attempt to get within one of the two major parties in the cities, they become co-opted and their interests are shunted to the background. They become expendable.

We must begin to think of the black community as a base of organization to control institutions in that community. Control of the ghetto schools must be taken out of the hands of "professionals," most of whom have long since demonstrated their insensitivity to the needs and problems of the black child. These "experts" bring with them middle-class biases, unsuitable techniques and materials; these are, at best, dysfunctional and at worst destructive. A recent study of New York schools reveals that the New York school system is run by thirty people—school supervisors, deputy and assistant superintendents and examiners. The study concluded: "Public education policy has become the province of the professional bureaucrat, with the tragic result that the status quo, suffering from many difficulties, is the order of the day." [1] Virtually no attention is paid to the wishes and demands of the parents, especially the black parents. This is totally unacceptable.

Black parents should seek as their goal the actual control of the public schools in their community: hiring and firing of teachers, selection of teaching materials, determination of standards, etc. This can be done with a committee of teachers. The traditional, irrelevant "See Dick, See Jane, Run Dick, Run Jane, White House, Nice Farm" nonsense must be ended. The principals and as many teachers as possible of the ghetto schools should be black. The children will be able to see their kind in positions of leadership and authority. It should never occur to anyone that a brand new school can be built in the heart of the black community and then given a white person to head it. The fact is that in this day and time, it is crucial that race be taken into account in determining policy of this sort. Some people will, again, view this as "reverse segregation" or as "racism." It is not. It is emphasizing race in a positive way: not to subordinate or rule over others but to overcome the effects of centuries in which race has been used to the detriment of the black man.

The story of I.S. 201 in New York City is a case in point. In 1958, the city's Board of Education announced that it would build a special $5-million school in District 4, whose pupils are ninety percent black, eight percent Puerto Rican, with the remaining two percent white. The concept was that students from elementary schools in that district would feed into the new school at the fifth grade and after the eighth grade would move on to high school. This concept, at least according to official policy, was supposed to speed integration.

[1] Marilyn Gittell, "Participants and Participation: A Study of School Policy in New York City," New York: The Center for Urban Education. As quoted in the *New York Times*, April 30, 1967, p. E90.

The parents of children who might be attending the school mobilized in an attempt, once and for all, to have a school adequate for the needs of Harlem. The Board had picked the site for I.S. 201: between 127th and 128th Streets, from Madison Avenue to Park Avenue—in the heart of Central Harlem. The parents argued against this location because they wanted an integrated school, which would be impossible unless it was located on the fringes, not in the heart, of Central Harlem. Their desire clearly points up the colonial relationship of blacks and whites in the city; they knew the only way to get quality education was to have white pupils in the school.

The Board of Education indicated that the school would be integrated, but the parents knew it could not be done and they demonstrated against the site during construction. When they saw that the school would have no windows, they also raised the question of whether this was merely a stylistic or practical innovation, or a means of closing out the reality of the community from the pupils for the hours they would be inside.

During the spring and summer of 1966, some six hundred pupils registered at I.S. 201—all of them black or Puerto Rican. Their parents then threatened that if the school wasn't integrated by fall, they would boycott it. The Board of Education, giving lip service to the parents, passed out and mailed 10,000 leaflets to the white community— in June!

Needless to say, few people go to a school on the basis of a leaflet received while getting off the subway or wherever, and even fewer (white) people want to send their children to school in Harlem. The request for "volunteers" had no effect, and on September 7, the Board of Education finally admitted its "apparent inability to integrate the school." It was the inability of that class described in Chapter VII, "whose primary interest is to secure objects for service, management, and control," the objects in this case being the mothers of I.S. 201. Threatened by a boycott, the school was not opened as scheduled on September 12, 1966.

At this point, the parents—who were picketing—moved in the only way they could: to demand some form of control which would enable them to break out of the old colonial pattern. In view of the fact that whites would not send their children to the school, one parent stated, "we decided we would have to have a voice to ensure that we got quality education segregated-style. We wanted built-in assurances." The parents knew that within a few years, given that pattern, this new school would be like all others which started with fine facilities and deteriorated under an indifferent bureaucracy. The parents' demands thus shifted fom integration to control.

On September 16, Superintendent Bernard E. Donovan offered them a voice in screening and recommending candidates for supervisory and teaching positions at the school. An East Harlem community council would be set up with a strong voice in school affairs. The parents also wanted some control over the curriculum, the career guidance system, and financial matters, which the Board deemed legally impossible. Shortly afterward, the white principal—Stanley Lisser—voluntarily requested transfer. A black principal had been one of the parents' key demands. With these two developments, the parents announced that they would send their children to school.

At this point (September 19), however, the United Federation of Teachers bolted. The teachers at I.S. 201 threatened to boycott if Lisser did not stay. Within twenty-four hours, the Board had rescinded its agreement and restored Lisser. (It is contended by many that this was the result of planned collusion between the Board and the U.F.T.) Nine days late, the school opened. The parents became divided; some gladly began sending their children to school while others did the same because they were unaware that the agreement had been rescinded.

The parents' negotiating committee had moved to get outside help, while the city's top administrators, including Mayor Lindsay, entered the picture. A Harlem committee representing parents and community leaders proposed on September 29 that I.S. 201 be put under a special "operations board" composed of four parents and four university educators with another member selected by those eight. This board would pass on the selection of teachers and supervisors, and evaluate the curriculum at I.S. 201 as well as three elementary or "feeder" schools. But the U.F.T. attacked this proposal. As the struggle dragged on, it became clear that once again efforts by the community to deal with its problems had been laid waste.

Later, in October, the Board of Education offered the parents a take-it-or-leave-it proposal. It proposed a council of parents and teachers that would be purely advisory. The parents flatly rejected this. Father Vincent Resta, a Catholic priest and chairman of the local school board which covered I.S. 201, stated, "In theory the Board's proposal is something that could work. But an advisory role implies trust. And this community has absolutely no reason to trust the Board of Education." The local board later resigned en masse.

But the issue of community control did not end there. It had become clear to the parents that their problems were not restricted to School District 4. When the Board of Education met to discuss its proposed budget in December, 1966, I.S. 201 parents and others came to protest the allocation of resources. Unable to get any response, at the end of one session they simply moved from the gallery into the chairs of those meeting and elected a People's Board of Education. After forty-eight hours, they were arrested and removed but continued to meet in another location, with the Rev. Milton A. Galamison—who had led school boycotts previously in New York City— as President.

At one of its executive sessions on January 8, 1967, the

People's Board adopted a motion which stated its goals as:

"1) To seek to alter the structure of the school system . . . so it is responsible to our individual community needs, in order to achieve real community control. This may require legislative or state constitutional convention action. This means, of course, decentralization, accountability, meaningful citizen participation, etc.

"2) To develop a program which will get grassroots awareness for, understanding of, and support for the goal stated above. It is suggested that we give top priority to organizing and educating parents and citizens in the poverty areas (approximately 14).

"3) That we recognize that power should not rest in any central board, including our own, and that by every means possible we should encourage the development and initiative of local people's groups."

The parents at I.S. 201 failed because they are still powerless. But they succeeded in heating up the situation to the point where the dominant society will have to make certain choices. It is clear that black people are concerned about the type of education their children receive; many more people can be activated by a demonstrated ability to achieve results. One result has already been achieved by the I.S. 201 struggle: the concept of community control has now rooted itself in the consciousness of many black people. Such control has long been accepted in smaller communities, particularly white suburban areas. No longer is it "white folks' business" only. Ultimately, community-controlled schools could organize an independent school board (like the "People's Board of Education") for the total black community. Such an innovation would permit the parents and the school to develop a much closer relationship and to begin attacking the problems of the ghetto in a communal, realistic way.

■

The tenements of the ghetto represent another target of high priority. Tenants in buildings should form cohesive organizations—unions—to act in their common interest vis-à-vis the absentee slumlord. Obviously, rents should be withheld if the owner does not provide adequate services and decent facilities. But more importantly, the black community should set as a prime goal the policy of having the owner's rights forfeited if he does not make repairs: forfeited and turned over to the black organization, which would not only manage the property but own it outright. The absentee slumlord is perpetuating a socially detrimental condition, and he should not be allowed to hide behind the rubric of property rights. The black community must insist that the goal of human rights take precedent over property rights, and back up that insistence in ways which will make it in the self-interest of the white society to act morally. Behavior—in this case, the misuse of property—can be regulated to any extent the power structure wishes. No one should be naïve enough to think that an owner will give up his property easily, but the black community, properly organized and mobilized, could apply pressure that would make him choose between the alternatives of forfeiture or compliance. Thousands of black people refusing to pay rents month after month in the ghettos could have more than a salutary effect on public policy.

■

As pointed out in Chapter I, virtually all of the money earned by merchants and exploiters of the black ghetto leaves those communities. Properly organized black groups should seek to establish a community rebate plan. The black people in a given community would organize and refuse to do business with any merchant who did not agree to "reinvest," say, forty to fifty percent of his net profit in the indigenous community. This contribution could take many forms: providing additional jobs for black people, donating scholarship funds for students, supporting certain types of community organizations. An agreement would be reached between the merchants and the black consumers. If a merchant wants customers from a black community, he must be made to understand that he has to contribute to that community. If he chooses not to do so, he will not be patronized, and the end result will be *no* profits from that community. Contractors who seek to do business in the black community would also be made to understand that they face a boycott if they do not donate to the black community.

Such a community rebate plan will require careful organization and tight discipline on the part of the black people. But it is possible, and has in fact already been put into effect by some ethnic communities. White America realizes the market in the black community; black America must begin to realize the potential of that market.

■

Under the present institutional arrangements, no one should think that the mere election of a few black people to local or national office will solve the problem of political representation. There are now ten black people on the City Council in Chicago, but there are not more than two or three (out of the total of fifty) who will speak out forcefully. The fact is that the present political institutions are not geared to giving the black minority an effective voice. Two needs arise from this.

First, it is important that the black communities in these northern ghettos form independent party groups to elect their own choices to office when and where they can. It should not be assumed that "you cannot beat City Hall." It has been done, as evidenced by the 1967 aldermanic elections in one of the tightest machine cities in the country: Chicago. In the Sixth Ward, an independent black candidate, Sammy Rayner, defeated an incumbent, machine-backed black alderman. Rayner first ran in 1963 and missed a run-off by a mere 177 votes. He then challenged Congressman William L. Dawson in 1964 and lost, but he was building an image in the black community as one who could and would speak out. The black people were getting the message. In 1967, when he ran against the machine incumbent for the City Council, he won handily. Precincts in the East Woodlawn area that he had failed to carry in 1963 (23 out of 26), he now carried (19 out of 26). The difference was continuous, hard, day-to-day, door-to-door campaigning. His campaign manager, Philip Smith, stated: "Another key to Sammy's victory was the fact that he began to methodically get himself around the Sixth Ward. Making the black club functions, attending youth meetings and all the functions that were dear to the hearts of Sixth Ward people became the order of the day." [2]

The cynics will say that Rayner will be just one voice, unable to accomplish anything unless he buckles under to the Daley machine. Let us be very clear: we do not endorse Rayner nor are we blind to the problems he faces. It is the job of the machine to crush such men or to co-opt them before they grow in numbers and power. At the same time, men like Rayner are useful only so long as they speak to the community's broad needs; as we said in Chapter II, black visibility is not Black Power. If Rayner does not remain true to his constituents, then they should dislodge him as decisively as they did his predecessor. This establishes the principle that the black politician must first be responsive to his constituents, not to the white machine. The problem then is to resist the forces which would crush or co-opt while building community strength so that more of such men can be elected and compelled to act in the community's interest.

[2] Philip Smith, "Politics as I See It," *The Citizen*, Chicago (March 22, 1967).

(It should be noted that Rayner is one of numerous black leaders who have rejected the term Black Power although their own statements, attitudes and programs suggest that they endorse what we mean by Black Power. The reason for this, by and large, is a fear of offending the powers-that-be which may go by the name of "tactics." This again exemplifies the need to raise the level of consciousness, to create a new consciousness among black people.)

The very least which Sammy Rayner can give the black community is a new political dignity. His victory will begin to establish the *habit* of saying "No" to the downtown bosses. In the same way that the black Southerner had to assert himself and say "No" to those who did not want him to register to vote, now the Northern black voter must begin to defy those who would control his vote. This very act of defiance threatens the status quo, because there is no predicting its ultimate outcome. Those black voters, then *accustomed* to acting independently, could eventually swing their votes one way or the other—but always for *their* benefit. Smith signaled this when he said: "The disbelievers who felt that you could not beat City Hall are now whistling a different tune. The victory of Sammy Rayner in the Sixth Ward should serve as a beacon light for all who believe in independent politics in this city. . . . Rayner is going to be responsible for the aldermanic position taking on a new line of dignity. Black people are going to be able to point with pride to this man, who firmly believes that we need statesmanlike leadership instead of the goatsmanship we have been exposed to." [3]

Let no one protest that this type of politics is naïve or childish or fails to understand the "rules of the game." The price of going along with the "regulars" is too high to pay for the so-called benefits received. The rewards of independence can be considerable. It is too soon to say precisely where this new spirit of independence could take

[3] *Ibid.*

us. New forms may lead to a new political force. Hopefully, this force might move to create new national and local political parties—or, more accurately, the first *legitimate* political parties. Some have spoken of a "third party" or "third political force." But from the viewpoint of community needs and popular participation, no existing force or party in this country has ever been relevant. A force which is relevant would therefore be a first—something truly new.

The second implication of the political dilemma facing black people is that ultimately they may have to spearhead a drive to revamp completely the present institutions of representation. If the Rayners are continually outvoted, if the grievances of the black community continue to be overlooked, then it will become necessary to devise wholly new forms of local political representation. There is nothing sacred about the system of electing candidates to serve as aldermen, councilmen, etc., by wards or districts. Geographical representation is not inherently right. Perhaps political interests have to be represented in some entirely different manner—such as community-parent control of schools, unions of tenants, unions of welfare recipients actually taking an official role in running the welfare departments. If political institutions do not meet the needs of the people, if the people finally believe that those institutions do not express their own values, then those institutions must be discarded. It is wasteful and inefficient, not to mention unjust, to continue imposing old forms and ways of doing things on a people who no longer view those forms and ways as functional.

We see independent politics (after the fashion of a Rayner candidacy) as the first step toward implementing something new. Voting year after year for the traditional party and its silent representatives gets the black community nowhere; voters then get their own candidates, but these may become frustrated by the power and organization of the machines. The next logical step is to demand more meaningful structures, forms and ways of dealing with long-standing problems.

■

We see this as the potential power of the ghettos. In a real sense, it is similar to what is taking place in the South: the move in the direction of independent politics—and from there, the move toward the development of wholly new political institutions. If these proposals also sound impractical, utopian, then we ask: what other real alternatives exist? There are none; the choice lies between a genuinely new approach and maintaining the brutalizing, destructive, violence-breeding life of the ghettos as they exist today. From the viewpoint of black people, that is no choice.

AFTERWORD:

◖ Whether one is talking about the fantastic changes taking place in Africa, Asia or the black communities of America, it is necessary to realize that the current, turbulent period in history is characterized by the demands of previously oppressed peoples to be free of their oppression. Those demands will not be quieted by guns or soft talk; those demands have a logic of their own—a logic frequently misunderstood by the oppressors. Those demands are part of the on-going process of modernization. We have described the essentially political aspects of that process among black people in America; we see independent politics as a crucial vehicle in our liberation. But at no

"T. C. B."

time must this development be viewed in isolation from similar demands heard around the world.

Black and colored peoples are saying in a clear voice that they intend to determine for themselves the kinds of political, social and economic systems they will live under. Of necessity, this means that the existing systems of the dominant, oppressive group—the entire spectrum of values, beliefs, traditions and institutions—will have to be challenged and changed. It is not to be expected that this fundamental scrutiny will be led by those who benefit or even have expectations of benefit from the status quo.

In this country, we therefore anticipate that the oppressed black people are the most legitimate and the most likely group to put the system to the test, to put the hard questions. Professor Kenneth B. Clark wrote: " . . . it is possible for an American Negro social psychologist to understand certain aspects of the American culture and the psychology of American whites with somewhat more clarity than is generally possible for whites who are accepted by and completely identified with this culture. . . . It is possible . . . that a Negro who has been trained in the discipline of the social sciences may be less influenced by certain subjective distortions which are operative in the American culture, or he may bring to his view of this culture certain counter-balancing distortions. The Negro in America, by virtue of the pervasive patterns of racial rejection, exclusion or a token and often self-conscious acceptance by a minority of white liberals, has been forced into a degree of alienation and detachment which has resulted in a pattern of social and personality consequences. Among these consequences has been sharpened insights and increased sensitivity to some of the subtle forces which are significant in our complex social structure." [1]

The victim of continued societal oppression brings to the situation a wholly different set of views of what is legitimate for change. The victim is more willing—much more willing—to risk the future, because he has very little to lose and a lot to gain. Obviously, this creates tremendous tensions, as the demands of a new group rub against the resistance of an old group. The old group, the settled, the secure, prefers peaceful, slow, moderate change. Frequently, of course, it prefers no change at all. But if change must come, then let it be in bits and pieces according to a time-

---

[1] Kenneth B. Clark, "What Motivates American Whites?" *Ebony* (August, 1965).

table predetermined by the old. The new group is on the make; it has visions of a new day, a rejuvenation, a release from poverty and oppression. And it does not take kindly to counsels of caution.

We cannot emphasize too much this relatively simple idea: that the two groups operate from different vantage points and different concepts of what constitutes legitimacy.

The old group admires stability and order. It calls for "cooling off" and "responsible action." It considers that the present activity could lead to unanticipated consequences which might be far worse than existing conditions. The new group rejects this and is willing to gamble on the future; the present is unacceptable.

Modernization is a time of dynamism when it is absolutely necessary to call for and push for new forms, new institutions to solve old problems. This call, this push requires a bold readiness to be "out of order." The prevailing social order is not capable of bold innovation in basic areas of life. White America is rich, strong, capable of grand designs to conquer space and other scientific feats, but it is woefully underdeveloped in its human and political relations. In these areas, it is primitive and backward. The advocates of Black Power serve to clarify this situation, to point out that advanced technology and a rising Gross National Product are not the only, or even the most important, indices of civilization. Black Power advocates help to modernize by puncturing the old theories, the old approaches, the well-worn clichés. Our function is to stress modernization, not moderation.

We are calling at this time for new political forms which will be the link between broadened participation (now occurring) and legitimate government. These forms will provide a means whereby a newly politicized people can get what they need from the government. It is not enough to add more and more people to the voter rolls and then send them into the old "do-nothing," compromise-oriented political parties. Those new voters will only become frustrated and alienated. It is no good to enact an anti-poverty program calling for "maximum feasible participation of the poor" and then saddle that program with old City Hall and bureaucratic restrictions. The people will see this only as a perpetuation of the same old colonial situation. This country can continue to appropriate money for programs to be run by the same kinds of insensitive people with paternalistic, Anglo-conformity attitudes and the programs will continue to fail. They should fail, because they do not have the confidence and trust of the masses. In order to gain that confidence and trust, the people must be much more involved in the formulation and implementation of policy. Black people are indeed saying: "Mr. Charlie, we'd rather do it ourselves." And in doing it themselves, they will be developing the *habit* of participation, the *consciousness* of ability to achieve, and the experience and wisdom to govern. Only this can ultimately create a viable body politic. It is not enough that shiny new school buildings be built in the ghettos, if the black people whose children attend them basically feel no attachment to those schools. Learning will not take place.

We have come to a stage in our history where the old approaches of doing *for* a people will no longer suffice. This is especially true when that which has been done often contributed to the retrogression, not the progression, of the recipients. No better example of this can be found than in the nation's welfare program. As Mitchell Ginsberg, director of New York City's Welfare Department, told a Senate sub-committee not long ago, the system is "bankrupt" as a social institution. Stating that the present system must be "thrown out" and calling for a new approach, he declared: "As long as public assistance does not perform its relief function in such a way as to free the poorest of the poor, rather than to lock them in dependency, it has failed as an anti-poverty weapon." [2]

Obviously, we must raise serious and basic questions about the overall role played by federal funds in relation to the black liberation struggle. Our basic premise is that money and jobs are not the final answer to the black man's problems. Without in any sense denying the overwhelming reality of poverty, we must affirm that the basic goal is not "welfare colonialism," as some have called the anti-poverty and other federal programs, but the inclusion of black people at all levels of decision-making. We do not seek to be mere recipients *from* the decision-making process but participants *in* it.

In any case, the fact is that any federal program conceived with black people in mind is doomed if blacks do not control it. The fact is that the government will never "give" blacks everything they need economically unless they have the power to threaten enough in order to get enough. The periodic hand-outs can never satisfy, even if they were desirable. It is our hope that the day may soon come when black people will reject federal funds because they have understood that these programs are geared to pacification rather than to genuine solutions. We hope that the rising level of consciousness may bring a rejection of such doles. This will strike many readers as fantastic, but they might recall that once in India, Gandhi rejected relief food shipments from England precisely because he saw them as tools of pacification.

At the same time, we recognize that experience with federal programs can, like the MFDP challenge experience with the Democratic party described in Chapter IV, serve as an education in control and bargaining, in the workings of the American system. Unintentionally, the government

[2] *The New York Times* (May 10, 1967), p. 1.

educates black people—provides them with a disillusion-
ment in that government and thereby breeds a new consciousness.

This kind of sophistication forms part of the black
consciousness which we see as vital to Black Power and to
the ending of racism. We understand the present rules
of the game and we reject them. But before the need for
new rules and new forms can be accepted by black people,
there must be created the will—the consciousness—for
those forms. One of the most promising developments in
the nation today is the new mood among black college
students, who have long formed a conservative group with
standard Horatio Alger dreams, imitating white America at
its worst. Agitation on black campuses in 1967 was profound and different from that of 1960–61: there is, today,
less of a moral and more of a political orientation. Humble
appeal is gone; a powerful mood has developed based on a
black consciousness. *The black intellectual is coming home*,
as black writer Eldridge Cleaver has suggested: "Up until
now, one of the traditional complaints of the black masses
has been of the treachery of black intellectuals . . . there
is a vast difference between Negroes who are willing to go
South and all those generations whose ambition was to flee
the South. A cycle has been completed. The real work for
the liberation of black people in America has begun." [3]

It is difficult, if not impossible, for white America, or
for those blacks who want to be like white America, to
understand this basically revolutionary mentality. But in
the final analysis, white America would save itself a lot of
trouble if it did try to understand and to come to terms
with this new black-oriented mentality. Because one thing
stands clear: whatever the consequences, there is a growing

[3] Eldridge Cleaver, "My Father and Stokely Carmichael," *Ramparts*
(April, 1967).

—a rapidly growing—body of black people determined to "T.C.B."—take care of business. They will not be stopped in their drive to achieve dignity, to achieve their share of power, indeed, to become their own men and women—in this time and in this land—by whatever means necessary.

■

BIBLIOGRAPHY

NOTE: *Many published works have helped the authors in the formulation of their ideas. Listed here are only those sources relevant to specific—generally, historical and factual—passages in this book.*

Apter, David, *The Politics of Modernization*, Chicago, University of Chicago Press, 1965.

Banfield, Edward C., *Big City Politics*, New York, Random House, 1965.

Banfield, Edward and Wilson, James Q., *City Politics*, New York, Random House (Vintage Books), 1966.

Bennett, Lerone, Jr., *Before the Mayflower: A History of the Negro in America, 1619–1962*, Chicago, Johnson Publishing Co., 1962.

Blumer, Herbert, "Race Prejudice as a Sense of Group Position," *Pacific Sociological Review*, Spring, 1958.

Brimmer, Andrew F., "The Negro in the National Economy," *The American Negro Reference Book* (ed. by John P. Davis), Englewood Cliffs, N.J., Prentice-Hall, 1966.

Caplovitz, David, *The Poor Pay More*, Glencoe, Ill., The Free Press, 1963.

Clark, Kenneth B., *Dark Ghetto*, New York, Harper & Row, 1965.

Drake, St. Clair and Cayton, Horace R., *Black Metropolis*, Vol. I, New York, Harper & Row (Harper Torchbooks), 1962.

DuBois, W. E. B., *Black Reconstruction in America*, New York, Meridian Books, 1964.

Fanon, Frantz, *The Wretched of the Earth*, New York, Grove Press, 1963.

Franklin, John Hope, *From Slavery to Freedom*, New York, Alfred A. Knopf, 1957.

Garfinkel, Herbert, *When Negroes March*, Glencoe, Ill., The Free Press, 1959.

Holt, Len, *The Summer that Didn't End*, New York, William Morrow, 1965.

Key, V. O., Jr., *Politics, Parties and Pressure Groups*, New York, Thomas Y. Crowell, 1964.

Killens, John O., *Black Man's Burden*, New York, Trident Press, 1965.

Killian, Lewis and Grigg, Charles, *Racial Crisis in America*, Englewood Cliffs, N.J., Prentice-Hall, 1964.

Kilson, Martin, *Political Change in a West African State, A Study of the Modernization Process in Sierra Leone*, Cambridge, Mass., Harvard University Press, 1966.

Meier, August and Rudwick, Elliot M., *From Plantation to Ghetto*, New York, Hill and Wang, 1966.

Morgenthau, Hans, *Politics among Nations*, New York, Alfred A. Knopf, 1966.

Nkrumah, Kwame, *Africa Must Unite*, London, Heinemann Educational Books, Ltd., 1963.

Scott, Emmett J. and Stowe, Lyman Beecher, *Booker T. Washington, Builder of a Civilization*, New York, Doubleday, Page & Co., 1917.

Silberman, Charles, *Crisis in Black and White*, New York, Random House, 1964.

Sorensen, Theodore, *Kennedy*, New York, Harper & Row, 1965.

Thompson, Daniel C., *The Negro Leadership Class*, Englewood Cliffs, N.J., Prentice-Hall, 1963.

Williams, Robin M., Jr., "Prejudice and Society," *The American*

Negro Reference Book (ed. by John P. Davis), Englewood Cliffs, N.J., Prentice-Hall, 1966.

Wilson, James Q., "The Negro in American Politics: The Present," *The American Negro Reference Book* (ed. by John P. Davis), Englewood Cliffs, N.J., Prentice-Hall, 1966.

Wilson, James Q., *Negro Politics*, Glencoe, Ill., The Free Press, 1960.

Woodward, C. Vann, *Tom Watson: Agrarian Rebel*, New York, Oxford University Press, 1963.

Young, Whitney, *To Be Equal*, New York, McGraw-Hill, 1964.

INDEX

191

ABOUT THE AUTHORS

STOKELY CARMICHAEL was born in Trinidad and grew up there, in New York City, and in Washington, D.C. He attended the Bronx High School of Science and received a bachelor's degree from Howard University in 1964. While at Howard he was active in student government, as well as in the local civil rights organization, the Nonviolent Action Group. Mr. Carmichael has worked with the Student Nonviolent Coordinating Committee almost since its inception in 1960. He has been arrested more than fifteen times while participating in demonstrations in Mississippi, Louisiana, Tennessee, Maryland, Virginia, and New York. Before his election as chairman of SNCC in May 1966, he helped organize the Lowndes County Freedom Organization in Alabama, and played a major role in the 1964 Mississippi Summer Project as director of civil rights activities in the Second Congressional District. Since the expiration of his term as SNCC chairman, Mr. Carmichael has been active in Black Power liberation activities in both North and South, with primary emphasis on ghetto organizing in Washington, D.C.

PROFESSOR CHARLES V. HAMILTON is chairman of the Department of Political Science at Roosevelt University in Chicago, from which he also received his B.A. In addition, he holds a law degree from Loyola University, and M.A. and Doctorate degrees from the University of Chicago. Professor Hamilton has taught at Tuskegee Institute, Albany State College (Georgia), Rutgers University (Newark), and Lincoln University. The author of a monograph titled "Minority Politics in Black Belt Alabama," he has also published articles on constitutional law and civil rights in the *Wisconsin Law Review*, *Phylon*, and the *Journal of Negro Education*. He has been both a participant in and advisor to civil rights organizations in Alabama, Georgia, Illinois, and Pennsylvania. Professor Hamilton, his wife, Dona, and their two daughters, Valli and Carol, make their home in Evanston, Illinois.

VINTAGE POLITICAL SCIENCE
AND SOCIAL CRITICISM

VINTAGE BIOGRAPHY AND AUTOBIOGRAPHY